THE ANTI-CHRISTIANITY OF KIERKEGAARD

THE ANTI-CHRISTIANITY OF KIERKEGAARD

A STUDY OF
CONCLUDING UNSCIENTIFIC POSTSCRIPT

by

HERBERT M. GARELICK
Rutgers, The State University

THE HAGUE / MARTINUS NIJHOFF / 1965

PRINTED IN THE NETHERLANDS

To My Mother and Father

ACKNOWLEDGMENTS

I should like to thank Frederick Sontag, Chairman of the Philosophy Department, Pomona College, for valuable criticisms of this manuscript. I should also like to thank Robert G. Olson, a colleague at Rutgers University, for very carefully reading an earlier version of this manuscript. Princeton University Press and Harper and Row very generously allowed me to quote from their works. In addition, I am grateful to the Rutgers University Research Council for a grant which enabled me to complete this work.

April, 1964   HERBERT M. GARELICK
                                                     New York City

CONTENTS

THE PROBLEM

Two approaches have characterized the study of Kierkegaard in English; the first is biographical, the second synoptic. Walter Lowrie, *Kierkegaard*, Eduard Geismar, *Lectures on the Religious Thoughts of Soren Kierkegaard*, Kurt Reinhardt, *The Existentialist Revolt*, and Theodor Haecker, *Kierkegaard, The Cripple*, all offer an understanding of Kierkegaard's position by reference to an analysis of his life and certain crucial experiences, especially the Regine affair.

James Collins, *The Mind of Kierkegaard*, R. Jolivet, *Introduction to Kierkegaard*, and Reidar Thomte, *Kierkegaard's Philosophy of Religion*, treat Kierkegaard synoptically, viewing his prodigious output as a seamless whole, gathering together in a single volume a discussion of all of his works and most of his problems.

The effect of these studies has become clearer in the last decades. There is an increasing sterility in Kierkegaardian scholarship, which, for the most part, focuses upon the elementary facts of Kierkegaard's life and basic themes of his system. Philosophic development and critical inspection are frozen in contemporary Kierkegaardian scholarship.

There are several reasons for this state. The very richness of Kierkegaard's life has drawn undue attention to itself rather than to his philosophic doctrines. It is always tempting to fasten upon Kierkegaard's life; its romantic phases demand attention. Furthermore, there is the fascination of rebellion by one of the great stylists of the nineteenth century. In Kierkegaard a literary style is put in the service of radical ideas in a stunning manner.

Still another difficulty is Kierkegaard's insistence upon action and his denegation of abstract thought: "Between the action as represented in thought on the one hand, and the real action on the other, between the possibility and the reality, there may in respect of content be no difference at all. But in respect of form, the difference is essential. Reality is the interest in action, in existence."[1] Since scholars usually live by talking or writing and not by acting, they hope to satisfy Kierkegaard's strictures by talking about acting and talking about commitment. In attempting to fulfill their devotion both to Kierkegaard and to their life work they succeed in satisfying neither. Kierkegaardian scholarship reacting to Kierkegaard's challenge tends to be exhortatory, visceral, and "edifying," pointing endlessly to the insights offered by Kierkegaard, hoping thereby to give the impression of action and commitment. Biography, which is much closer to "life" than speculation, becomes the favored treatment of Kierkegaard. This, when augmented by an exposition of major themes in Kierkegaard, has the purpose of wangling from the reader commitment, and, incidentally, justification for writing about Kierkegaard. But attempting to color theory to resemble life does justice neither to theory nor to life. "Green is life, grey is theory," as the devil so wisely said; when faced with this dichotomy, Kierkegaardian scholars, by retreating to biography and popularization, choose neither theory nor life and thus compromise both.

Another reason for the present state of Kierkegaardian criticism is the extreme fluidity of his system. Its ambiguities, digressions, pseudonyms, and sheer size of output overwhelm the imagination. Kierkegaard's warning, "... that no half-learned man would lay a dialectic hand upon this work, but would let it stand as now it stands," [2] is sufficient to restrain all but the most determined. Here, though, a misunderstanding is involved. Kierkegaard asks to be taken seriously; he makes assertions and offers reasons for them. Nowhere does he ask that no critical word disturb the results, but that only the dilettante and the passionless desist: "... suppose that Christianity is subjectivity, an inner transformation, an actualization of inwardness, and that only two kinds of people can know anything about it: those who with an infinite passionate interest in an eternal happiness base this their happiness upon their believing relationship to Christianity, and those who with an opposite passion, but in passion, reject it – the happy and unhappy lovers. Suppose than an objective indifference can therefore learn nothing at all. Only the like is understood by the like..." [3]

---

[1] S. Kierkegaard, *Concluding Unscientific Postscript*, Princeton, N.J., Princeton University Press, 1941, p. 304.
[2] *Postscript*, pp. 553–4.
[3] *Postscript*, p. 51.

Surely it is a mark of greater respect to examine a doctrine and by that examination discern its infinite implications than to stand in mute silence before the word alone.

The dangers of the present impasse in Kierkegaardian scholarship are clear. A philosophically fruitful dialogue resulting in criticism which increases understanding is absent. Yet to talk and to break with talk are decisions. They follow from reasons, either consciously or unconsciously held. Despite a flood of radical statements passionately uttered, and seemingly hastily written, few in the nineteenth century worked longer over their reasons for acting than Kierkegaard. To ignore his reasons, to refuse to discuss them critically, and to focus only upon his conclusions is to misunderstand him. Christian faith is possible only to one who understands: "Every man, the wisest and the simplest, can qualitatively... distinguish just as essentially between what he understands and what he does not understand,... and he can discover that there is something which is, in spite of the fact that it is against his understanding and way of thinking. When he stakes his life upon this absurd, he makes the motion in virtue of the absurd, *and he is essentially deceived in case the absurd he has chosen can be proved to be not the absurd.*" [1] To skip justification and argument and ignore reason in Kierkegaard is to lose both his subjectivity and his Christianity. To act in ignorance is not to act *against* reason; acting against understanding is required: "So it is also in the case of one who is really a Christian... He may very well have understanding (indeed he must have it in order to believe against understanding)..." [2]

Further: "The realm of faith is thus not a class for numbskulls in the sphere of the intellectual, or an asylum for the feebleminded." [3] Christianity requires the highest use of reason and obligates us to examine the religious act: "... if we overlook the dialectical factor [understanding], what happens? Why then the whole affair becomes mere prattle and old wives' bawling; for Jews and women, as we all know, can bawl out more in a single minute than a man can accomplish in an entire lifetime..." [4] It simply will not do to concentrate upon Regine. What is needed is a philosophic examination and criticism of Kierkegaard's position.

The task of examining Kierkegaard's work philosophically is not

---

[1] *Postscript*, p. 495–6 (italics added).
[2] *Postscript*, p. 503.
[3] *Postscript*, p. 291.
[4] *Postscript*, p. 385.

easy. It is only on the basis of an investigation of individual problems and a study of particular works that gives us warrant to pass judgments upon Kierkegaard's total work, a field now pre-empted by those who deal in generalizations and often without scrupulous reference to a text, which, often enough, is ambiguous and difficult to interpret even within the particular work in which it occurs.

I have followed the tradition set by Emil Hirsch in *Kierkegaard-Studien* and have started with a philosophic investigation of one work, *Concluding Unscientific Postscript*, and one philosophic problem, Kierkegaard's definition of "Christian" in the *Postscript*. This study considers the problem as to what constitutes a religious person, more specifically, what it means to become a Christian. This is not to be confused with the problem of the many ways in which "religious" or "Christian" may be defined. The history of the definition of these terms is not relevant; what is important is making clear what Kierkegaard means by religion and Christianity as a unique mode of being, separate and distinct from other ways of life, and then to investigate whether his explanation is coherent and meaningful within his own philosophy.

With the understanding of Kierkegaard's definition of "religious" and "Christian" some interesting results follow. In the *Postscript* Kierkegaard, in the persona of Climacus claims existence to be non-rational or not understandable in rational systems, and that religion, and Christianity in particular, is the irrational element in a non-rational life. Yet Climacus succeeds only in demonstrating that life, religion, and Christianity finally are dominated by the image of reason. It is the Paradox, the absolute center of Christianity for Climacus, defined by him as the Irrational, which reveals the power reason has over man.

My thesis, then, has three parts: (1) Climacus defines Christianity as irrational. (2) It is not; his definition involves an interesting dependence upon reason. (3) Consequently, there is a cunning backsliding in Climacus's notion of Christianity. While claiming Christianity to be the essence of irrationality and thereby drawing upon the Christian the highest suffering in violating common sense and reason, Climacus' Christianity becomes a clever device to avoid difficult existential problems such as death and meaninglessness.

Opposition to this thesis is great: (1) That Climacus defines Christianity as the irrational is denied by such scholars as N. H. Søe, James Collins, Cornelio Fabro, C.P.S., and J. Heywood Thomas.

Søe:

Kierkegaard in fact asserts that the concept of "the absurd" is the "negative criterion of that which is higher than human reason, and human knowledge." The task of reason is to demonstrate that such is the case – "and then to leave it to each individual to decide whether he will believe it or not" (X6B 80). In view of this, one should assume that for Kierkegaard the "paradox" is an expression for what is *supra rationem* rather than for what is *contra rationem*.[1]

Collins:

Kierkegaard sometimes speaks as though the intellect were positively excluded from the act of faith. Yet all that his opposition to idealism and pantheism requires is that faith not be regarded as the necessary outcome of a demonstrative process, in which reason alone is operative. He uses the weapon of intelligence to defend the irreducible distinction between the finite individual and God. This suggests that there are other ways of viewing the intellect than the one dictated by the presuppositions of Hegelianism.[2]

Fabro:

Meanwhile, the work of reason is not excluded from the object of faith as such, although it operates certainly not in order to explain it but in order to prepare and invite man in some way to accept it. Moreover, reason is able to establish that the object of faith transcends reason and cannot depend on it. Kierkegaard has coined the formula "to understand that it is impossible to understand" which recalls, as he himself notices, St. Thomas' maxim "nothing can be at the same time known and believed." The *Postscript*, which mainly deals with this problem, expresses at the same time the absolute heterogeneity of reason and faith and the possibility of the former coming to recognize the transcendence of the latter through a certain knowledge of cause.

In his maturity, Kierkegaard re-examined the content and meaning of the *Postscript* and gave them further precision in the way shown above, arriving at the express recognition of the possibility of theological speculation, naturally in subordination to faith. Christianity is communication of existence and not only a new doctrine. According to Kierkegaard, the first movement of the Christian consciousness goes from faith to faith, always within faith. But in the benevolence which is its characteristic, Christianity also allows the use of reason provided that it does not go beyond its own limits and that it be satisfied to understand that it is impossible to understand and must not understand.[3]

Thomas:

Obviously it is futile to ask for a belief in something ridiculous. It is impossible to imagine a person saying, "I believe the moon is a green cheese" – or at any rate if we ever came across someone who said this we would know what to do with him! This is what Kierkegaard has said already; that just any absurdity is not good enough here. It is an absurd that must be true. It must make sense

---

[1] N. H. Søe, "Kierkegaard's Doctrine of the Paradox," in Howard Johnson and Niels Thulstrup, editors, *A Kierkegaard Critique*, New York, Harper & Row, 1962, p. 209.

[2] James Collins, "Faith and Reflection in Kierkegaard," in *A Kierkegaard Critique*, p. 150.

[3] Cornelio Fabro, C.P.S., "Faith and Reason in Kierkegaard's Dialetic," in *A Kierkegaard Critique*, pp. 177–80.

when we have believed. We have seen quite clearly that the contradiction must not be played down. Here more than anywhere in Christianity we must *believe*. It is usually said of Tertullian that he made the Christian faith a fluid faith in paradox. What is probably the truth is that he grasped this point, that faith believed where it *could not* know. Kierkegaard repeats the salutary lesson that *credo* means *nescio, sed credo quia absurdum est objectum fidei*. This is the leap through the possibility of offence. Once on the other side, though, we see the meaningfulness and truth of the absurd so that it is no longer for us the absurd.[1]

(2) That Kierkegaard attempts to postulate Christianity as irrational and fails to do so is denied by the aforementioned scholars as well as by E. L. Allen, who finds Kierkegaard to be thoroughly irrational.

Allen:

Few men have offered to God such a sacrifice as he did, yet surely that he gave was that one sacrifice which God does not ask of His children, for it was the quenching of the Inner Light.[2]

(3) That Climacus' Christianity, rather than the cause of the greatest suffering, offers the only rational and easy solution to men's problems goes against almost the whole of Kierkegaardian scholarship. James Collins, H. V. Martin, Martin Heinecken, Marie Thulstrup, and H. R. Macintosh are united in their insistence upon the Kierkegaardian conception of Christianity as involving great suffering.

Collins:

The "category of suffering" is employed catastrophically in the religious sphere to dissolve the illusion of Christendom, just as the category of the individual is used in social matters to break the power of the irresponsible crowd. Kierkegaard's strategy is to quote at its very highest the price of becoming a Christian, stressing the severity of the test which must be passed, rather than the consolation which follows.[3]

Martin:

The absolute paradox, in which form the Christian revelation is presented, acts as a repulsive power against the natural immediacy of faith. Thus the act of faith in Christ has to be a decision, an act of the will, a plunge and a leap to which man comes only after an intense inward struggle.[4]

Heinecken:

The suffering of the Christian is for Kierkegaard not something accidental which comes and goes with the varying fortunes of life, just as dread is for him not

---

[1] J. Heywood Thomas, *Subjectivity and Paradox*, Oxford, Basil Blackwell, 1957, p. 133.
[2] E. L. Allen, *Kierkegaard, His Life and Thought*, London, Nott, 1935, p. 22.
[3] James Collins, *The Mind of Kierkegaard*, London, Secker and Warburg, 1954, p. 220.
[4] H. V. Martin, *The Wings of Faith*, New York, Philosophical Library, 1951, p. 88.

something accidental occasioned by intermittent encounter with the fear-arousing. Dread is a constant accompaniment of human existence, and so also is suffering a constant concomitant of being a Christian.[1]

Thulstrup:

Therefore, the meaning of life, according to Kierkegaard, is to be found in the possibility of suffering. One cannot avoid suffering when the eternal and the temporal collide. Suffering is, therefore, the distinctive mark which indicates that the collision has taken place.[2]

Macintosh:

... by insisting on irrational paradox he seeks to bring out the indubitable element of provocactiveness in the Gospel – what the New Testament calls "the *offence* of the Cross." In the Gospel as apostles preached it there is to be found something which, as we say familiarly, is more than nature can bear. It scandalizes both reason and moral common sense.[3]

As against these scholars I shall demonstrate my thesis in the following way: I expound Climacus' position in the *Postscript*, attempting by the use of quotation and analysis of text to show Climacus' position. I then show that Climacus necessarily uses and never abandons the reason he claims to be able to deny in the Paradox, and finally, to suggest that no one can escape reason. Much criticism of Kierkegaard finds him to be anti- or non-Christian on the basis of the critics' definition of Christianity. On the contrary, this study shows that Climacus' own definition of Christianity is self-referentially inconsistent; in suggesting a definition of Christianity as irrational, Climacus actually defines Christianity as rational. The demonstration of this proceeds by an analysis of the major concepts of the *Postscript*, which is crucial in understanding Kierkegaard's Christianity. The *Postscript* occupies a central position in his works, all dominated by one problem: what it means to become Christian. The *Postscript*, however, never fully states a final Christian position, Kierkegaard not quite lending his own name to the work. Works not specifically representing his final Christian viewpoint were written under a pseudonym.[4] The *Postscript*, having been written by "Johannes Climacus," is, then, not fully Christian nor was it meant to be. However, having given out Climacus

---

[1] Martin J. Heinecken, *The Moment Before God*, Philadelphia, Muhlenberg Press, 1956, p. 291.
[2] Marie Thulstrup, "Kierkegaard's Dialectic of Imitation," in *A Kierkegaard Critique*, pp. 273–4.
[3] H. R. Macintosh, *Types of Modern Theology*, London, Nisbet and Co., 1954, p. 245.
[4] S. Kierkegaard, *The Point of View for My Work as An Author: A Report to History*, New York, Harper & Row, 1962, p. 12.

as author on the title page, we find immediately below it: "Responsible for Publication: S. Kierkegaard." As Kierkegaard moves his name closer to actual authorship his works come closer to his final position; the *Postscript* is to be seen as an approach to a final understanding of what a Christian is. It contains an ingenious philosophic defense of Christianity. Arguments are held by Climacus which lead to an extremely subtle view of the nature of religion, put forward, for the most part, under the guise of no argument.

The *Postscript* is also, by design, a non-Christian work. Climacus is not Christian, not being able to make the final leap, that is, to relate himself absolutely to the absurd idea of the God-man. He is only a humorist: "The Undersigned, Johannes Climacus, who has written this book, does not give himself out to be a Christian; he is completely taken up with the thought how difficult it must be to be a Christian... He is a humorist; content with his situation at this moment, hoping that something higher may be granted him...[1] A humorist, however, is one who understands what is required of a Christian even if he is unable to meet its demands: "The humorist constantly... sets the God-idea into conjunction with other things and evokes the contradiction – but he does not maintain a relationship to God in terms of religious passion *stricte sic dictus*, he transforms himself instead into a jesting and yet profound exchange-center for all these transactions, but he does not himself stand related to God. The religious man does the same, he sets the God-idea into juxtaposition with everything and sees the contradiction, but in his inmost consciousness he is related to God."[2] Thus Climacus is not a "pagan" even if not a Christian; he claims to understand Christianity and what is required of the Christian: "He touches upon the secret of existence in the pain, but then he goes home again."[3]

But further it is my thesis that Climacus neither makes the final movement to Christianity *nor* understands Christianity properly. This is the anti-Christian element of the *Postscript*. Thus the *Postscript* is a profoundly anti-Christian work in a way certainly not intended by the "author" Climacus, who admits only to not being able to fulfill the movement to Christianity, but who claims to understand what is required of a Christian.

Whether the *Postscript* is anti-Christian in a way that was intended

---

[1] *Postscript*, p. 544.
[2] *Postscript*, p. 451.
[3] *Postscript*, p. 400.

by Kierkegaard, and thus Climacus made to serve as a warning to the reader, or whether the anti-Christian conclusion can be attributed to Kierkegaard as well as Climacus, I find a fascinating problem. The solution, however, lies outside of the *Postscript* and thus outside of the scope of this work. Important religious arguments and an anti-Christian conclusion are, at the very least, attributable to Climacus; I want to discuss these within the context of the *Postscript*. My purpose is to show the importance of the *Postscript* for an understanding of religion and Christianity.

This study proceeds by an analysis of the major themes developed in the *Postscript*: (1) A critique of reason. (2) The concept of subjectivity. (3) The nature of the paradox. (4) The Christianity of the *Postscript*. (5) The anti-Christianity of the *Postscript*. I define "Christian" as Climacus does when presenting what he regards as true Christianity (chapter 4), and then show how important elements in Climacus' thought conflict with his definition of Christianity as well as with the orthodox definition. Chapters 2 and 3 expound the concepts necessary to understand the problems encountered in the *Postscript* and the answers given by Climacus. I then show the contribution he makes to philosophic theology by his treatment of the Paradox (chapter 4), and chapters 5 and 6, judge the success of Climacus' efforts.

CHAPTER 2

A CRITIQUE OF REASON

Arguments against reason have had a long tradition in philosophy beginning with the skeptics and continuing to our century with Henri Bergson. I shall expound arguments against reason used by Climacus, and then attempt to show their importance to his thought.

Reason is unable to deal with problems of existence. Climacus in his critique of reason first examines the limits of language and communication, the vehicle by which reason is conveyed. There are four criticisms of language.

(1) Direct, external communication between man and man transforms an incomplete, inner dialogue of the individual into concrete conclusions and results. A third element, communication, is imposed between the individual and his concern; it tends to become the focus of attention. It displaces the proper binary relationship and converts the process of inner dialogue into a result. Where previously an individual and his concern were essential, the relation between an individual and his words now becomes essential. Language communicates consequences and conclusions successfully; however, it fails to transmit processes of existence or inner states of feeling. As Climacus says: "Suppose a man wished to communicate the conviction that it is not the truth but the way which is the truth, i.e. that the truth exists only in the process of becoming, in the process of appropriation, and hence that there is no result. Suppose he were a philanthropic soul who simply had to proclaim this to all and sundry; suppose he hit upon the excellent short cut of communicating it in a direct form through the newspapers, thus winning masses of adherents, while the artistic way would in spite of his utmost exertions have left it undetermined whether he had helped anyone or not: what then? Why then his principle would have turned out to be precisely a result."[1]

[1] S. Kierkegaard, *Concluding Unscientific Postscript*, Princeton, N.J., Princeton University Press, 1941, p. 72.

The direct form of communication gives only results – and results are "rubbish." Communication, to be effective in existence, must be indirect. The *indirect* form of communication is not, however, another more encompassing language system which can carry existence and feelings. It is a series of negative hints in language designed to drive us away from language. Through irony and humor, we are forced from language to a confrontation and a personal appropriation: "... the art of *communication* at last becomes the art of *taking away*, of luring something away from someone."[1]

(2) To convey something unique, something *sui generis*, we are compelled to communicate it in the same form, using the same words as in ordinary conversation. Any attempt to express the truly different is to make it trivial. Language, which is used to express everything, forbids the meaningful statement of that which claims to be absolutely apart from everything. It can give the unique only as much weight as everything else; the numinous of feeling is thereby negated. Existence, itself a unique *sui generis*, is reduced to the trivial and commonplace by communication. Climacus says: "That such a paragraph [one which attempts to convey existence] is a mockery of the entire system, that instead of being a paragraph in a system it is an absolute protest against the system, makes no difference to busy systematists. If the concept of existence is really to be stressed, this cannot be given a direct expression as a paragraph in a system: all direct swearing and oath-supported assurances serve only to make the topsy-turvy profession of the paragraph more and more ridiculous."[2]

(3) The third failure of ordinary communication is that it necessarily and helpfully foreshortens existence but at a prohibitive cost to certain feelings and qualities of existence. The value of language is its abstractness, that is, its abridgement of space and time. Discourse is valuable because it does not duplicate living processes but abstracts from them in the form of counters or symbols which stand for these living processes. Language is useless when attempting to emulate existence. Furthermore, it is absurd to assert that language can reproduce existence literally, if only because of the limitations of space and time imposed by the language system itself. To solve problems and to come to conclusions, it is necessary to manipulate reality by moving symbols of it at will and arranging them in imaginative ways. Discourse

---

[1] *Postscript*, p. 72.
[2] *Postscript*, p. 111.

must always be more abstract than existence; it gives a foreshortened perspective and therein derives its value.

But this dessication of space and time creates a necessary and in-alienable difference between language and the quality and texture of experience; it radically converts the truth of that experience. No matter what wordiness one may use in embroidering the statement: "For five years I have been suffering," it will always be infinitely easier for one to say than *be*. Language condenses; but existence is a continued persistence in unabridged space and time; to translate one into the other is to lose the quality of becoming. Existence is measured by our continued moment by moment responses. Here the foreshort-ened perspective given by language fails us by necessarily minimizing the breadth and thickness of the existential experience. Climacus says: "... speech is after all a more abstract medium than existence, and all speech in relation to the ethical is something of a deception, because discourse, in spite of the most subtle and thoroughly thought out precautionary measures, still always retains an appearance of the fore-shortened perspective. So that even when the discourse makes the most enthusiastic and desperate exertions to show how difficult it is, or attempts its utmost in an indirect form, it always remains more difficult to do it than it seems to be in the discourse."[1]

(4) Finally, languages forces distinctions upon existence where there are none. Breadth in existence is all. Language breaks up the unity in existence: "The subjective thinker has a form, a form for his com-munication with other men, and this form constitutes his style. It must be as manifold as the opposites he holds in combination. The systematic *ein, zwei, drei* is an abstract form, and must therefore fail when applied to the concrete."[2] In more complete form the argument is stated in *Johannes Climacus*. Before the maturation of speech there is an immediacy – a general indefiniteness in which even opposites reside comfortably:

How then is the child's consciousness to be described? It is essentially quite indefinite, a fact we can also state by saying that it is "immediate." *Immediacy is indefiniteness*. In immediacy relationships are absent; for as soon as relation-ships exist, immediacy is annulled. *In immediacy therefore everything is true;* but this truth is straightway untrue; for *in immediacy everything is untrue*, [because not reflected upon. What is outside reflection is as much true as untrue – till we reflect]. If consciousness can remain in immediacy then the whole question of truth is done away.[3]

---

[1] *Postscript*, p. 414.
[2] *Postscript*, p. 319
[3] S. Kierkegaard, *Johannes Climacus*, or, *De Omnibus Dubitandum Est*, Stanford, Calif., Stanford University Press, 1958, p. 147.

Speech arbitrarily invokes distinctions in the prejudgmental whole by using symbols to represent arbitrarily selected aspects of immediacy. "That which annuls immediacy therefore is speech. If man could not speak, then he would remain in immediacy. J. C. thought this might be expressed by saying that immediacy is reality and speech is ideality. For when I speak, I introduce opposition."[1]

Thus, a distinction and opposition between immediacy and the world of symbols is created. The symbols are not immediacy; they express parts of it, but particular, differentiated symbols cannot express what is neither particular nor differentiated. Through speech we force distinctions, creating a realm of "truth" on the verbal level which is an arbitrary reconstruction of immediacy.

If truth is a creation of the mind or speech and not of the immediate, so also is error or untruth just such an artificial creation. The immediate is just that, the immediate; it cannot deceive us or cause us to err. Judgments of "true" or "non-true" are not themselves accurate of the undifferentiated whole; they are the creation of speech operating on that whole, causing immediacy to be other than it is.

With the maturation and use of reason and speech a movement away from immediacy begins, for reason rejects as contradictory that immediacy whose main feature is a chaotic indefiniteness; reason then finds solace only in the consistency of its own terms. The reduction of all immediacy to the principle of non-contradiction is the function of reason; it is a state artificially created by a reason which denies and loses interest in the immediate from which it has arisen. Just as much of Eastern thought, particularly Taoism, has done away with one factor, reason, in facing the problem of the conflict between the two realms, so Western Rationalist philosophy makes the opposite mistake, removing the other half of the dichotomy, existence. The consequence is our divorce through reason from existence and immediacy itself.

To value reason and language as the judge of experience is to end with and only with reason. By its endless process of symbol manufacture, reason creates an opposition between the immediate and symbols, which it then solves by denying the immediate. By fragmenting the immediate, speech and reason gain important practical advantages; however, in doing so we lose experience.

The arguments Climacus uses against language are part of his critique of reason. Reason fails in meeting existential problems in three

[1] *Johannes Climacus*, p. 148.

ways: (1) Reason entails infinite regress. (2) Reason offers only possibility in matters that demand certainty. (3) Reason distorts the process nature of reality.

(1) Reason does not allow us to come to a decision culminating in action. Every authentic action can take place only after a break with reason. Reason is infinite; any attempt to secure the foundations of its thought must have a justification. But a justification of that justification is necessary before we begin truly. But this too needs justification, and so on *ad infinitum*. No final resting place is to be found; there is no self-justified beginning. Consequently, as Epictetus said, reflection is endless; action is lost.

In living, decision and action are necessary; we do not have endless time in which to contemplate. Reason, infinitely contemplative, can never come to a justified decision culminating in action. Since it is always possible to reflect one step more, decisions are rationally postponed. In order to act we must, therefore, break with reason: "Only when reflection comes to a halt can a beginning be made, and reflection can be halted only by something else, and this something else is something quite different from the logical, being a resolution of the will."[1] To act is to break out of objective reason in an arbitrary manner.

(2) If speculative reason fails, so also does historical knowledge. This knowledge is a branch of the speculative containing the same flaw of infinite regress. In addition it yields only possibility where certainty is required.

An example of the failure peculiar to historical knowledge is illustrated by an examination of the historical evidence for Christianity. Assume we have the best evidence that Jesus lived, that miracles were performed which were witnessed by trustworthy persons, and that there was a Resurrection, also carefully witnessed. Assume Christianity were to lay claim to truth on the most rigorous historical evidence. But this could not establish its truth. Historical knowledge is based on the assumption that sense evidence is trustworthy; yet, as is obvious, sense knowledge is fallible: "The study of Greek scepticism is much to be recommended. There one may learn thoroughly... that the certainty of sense perception, to say nothing of historical certainty, is uncertainty, is only an approximation."[1]

Since at best sense knowledge is only probable or approximate and since Christianity claims to be eternally true, no mode of knowledge

---

[1] *Postscript*, p. 103.
[2] *Postscript*, p. 38.

yielding probability at most can establish an absolute truth: "When Christianity is viewed from the standpoint of its historical documentation, it becomes necessary to secure an entirely trustworthy account of what the Christian doctrine really is... for nothing is more readily evident than that the greatest attainable certainty with respect to anything historical is merely an *approximation*. And an approximation, when viewed as a basis for an eternal happiness is wholly inadequate..."[1] Historical knowledge is only probable; it will not enable us to authenticate the claim of the Eternal and Absolute – if there is any.

(3) In opposition to the introduction of movement into logic by means of a transition category Climacus offers his major argument against reason's ability to meet existential problems.

Existence is change, process, or movement; reason cannot allow change, process, or movement; therefore reason is unable to deal with existence: "It is impossible to conceive existence without movement, and movement cannot be conceived *sub specie aeterni*."[2]

The laws of contradiction, identity, and excluded middle, necessary to reason and language, prevent reason from catching movement. In reason and language everything is what it is, and not another ($\sim$ (P $\cdot \sim$ P)). In becoming, nothing is, yet, becoming is not nothing. Becoming is something before it is what it is. But to assert this movement is to contradict ourselves, for, by our logical and linguistic construction, we make movement, process, and becoming itself something. Therefore becoming, by the edicts of logic, (A is A), (A $\vee \sim$ A), $\sim$ (A $\cdot \sim$ A), is what it is and not another. But a thing that is what it is and not another is not in a state of movement. Through reason we reduce existence to frozen states of being; given the law of contradiction it is impossible to explain the movement from one frozen state to another. Abstraction, by its analysis of movement into immobile categories and phases, robs existence of its existence. It is reduced to a state of being, "x," which occupies a certain space at a certain time, $T_1 \ldots T_2 \ldots T_3$ with only the miracle of the word "dialectic" to get us from T_1 to T_2. Reason operates on existence, dividing movements into parts. But movement is neither parts nor the collection of such parts; movement cannot be divided or analyzed without destroying that movement.

Climacus' challenge to the rationalist tradition is directed against

---

[1] *Postscript*, p. 25.
[2] *Postscript*, p. 273.

the illegal attempt to introduce movement in a sphere where movement is automatically reified. This rationalist position asserts that thought can explain existence. Anselm's ontological proof states this thesis. Its formula: our being able to think of Perfection entails admitting its existence. Climacus' answer: thought necessitates nothing – other than thought itself, which is empty of existence.

Climacus' argument against rationalism is a repetition of Zeno's paradoxes, with one exception: For Zeno since motion cannot be understood rationally there can be no motion. For Climacus since becoming cannot be understood rationally reason is to be rejected as the arbiter of existence. If one accepts reason, then time, movement, and motion are illusory. By making the intellectual criterion supreme, becoming or process is, then, denied. When reason is made the criterion of existence, reason is the only element that escapes criticism: "Reflection has the remarkable property of being infinite. But to say that it is infinite is equivalent, in any case, to saying that it cannot be stopped by itself; because in attempting to stop itself it must use itself, and is thus stopped in the same way that a disease is cured when it is allowed to choose its own treatment, which is to say that it waxes and thrives."[1]

The dissolution of existence and reason's endurance are the inevitable and *valid* consequences of using our reason. The presupposition, however, that reason ought to be the ultimate criterion is neither necessary nor justified. Zeno's conclusions are justified – if reason is made the arbiter of experience; but the bias for reason is arbitrary: "The infinite preponderance which the logical as the objective has over all thinking, is again limited by the fact that seen subjectively it is an hypothesis."[2]

Although accepting Zeno's analysis, his conclusion is reversed by Climacus; instead of rejecting existence because it is proved to be contradictory, Climacus rejects reason because it proves existence to be self-contradictory. By using reason we end with nothing more than reason. If we choose not to certify reason as the ultimate criterion of existence, we are once again in existence.

Climacus' critique of reason and language avoids the self-referential inconsistency of those who attack the validity of reason with reason. To say there are no valid rational truths and therefore we are free to reject reason is to assert at least two presumably rational truths; namely, that there are none, and that *because* there are none we are

1 *Postscript*, p. 101.
2 *Postscript*, p. 100.

permitted to abandon reason. Every denial of the validity of reason is an affirmation of the validity of reason.

Reaffirmation in denial is for Plato and Aristotle the sign of the eternal validity of reason; to attempt rationally to deny reason presupposes the validity of the reason one denies. It is this endurance of reason, its self-justification, that marks the absolute necessity and validity of reason. Reaffirmation in denial is shown in two ways: (a) In the truth claim made by the assertions which attempt to deny reason. (b) In the structure of language which carries meaning to be communicated.

(a) For Plato the eternal validity of reason could not be denied. Every assertion affirms its own truth even when the assertion denies all truth. As against Protagoras who claims there is no objective reason, but that all truth is relative and subjective, Socrates points out the inconsistency of this view. To attribute no validity to reason leads to the denial of the truth of one's own thesis, thereby robbing that thesis of any compulsion. Aristotle, too, is scornful of those who forget the truth claim they make whenever an assertion is made. The person denying reason does in fact profess it in the authority of his assertion; thus the only alternative to affirming the eternal validity of reason and the law of contradiction would be silence, represented by Cratylus who hoped to affirm complete relativity by silence while wagging his little finger. But such a man is not even human, being reduced to a vegetable existence.

(b) The argument, however, takes a decisive turn in Aristotle. He shows the impossibility of denying reason by an analysis of linguistic structure. Language is the vehicle by which all statements are carried; if the vehicle demands rationality, the material it carries must also conform to that demand. Reason's eternal validity is affirmed because any attempt to deny reason must employ reason and the laws of logic in constructing sentences which have meaning:

Thus in the first place it is obvious that this at any rate is true; that the term "to be" or "not to be" has a definite meaning; so that not everything can be "so and not so." Again, if "man" has one meaning, let this be "two-footed animal." By "has one meaning" I mean this: if X means "man," then if anything is a man, its humanity will consist in being X. And it makes no difference even if it be said that "man" has several meanings, provided that they are limited in number; for one could assign a different name to each formula. For instance, it might be said that "man" has not one meaning but several, one of which has the formula "two-footed animal," and there might be many other formulae as well, if they were limited in number; for a particular name could be assigned to each formula. If on the other hand it be said that "man" has an infinite number of meanings, obviously there can be no discourse; for not to have one meaning is to have no meaning, and if words have no meaning there is an end of discourse with others, and even, strictly speaking, with oneself; because it is impossible to think of anything if we do not think of one thing...[1]

The conclusion, then, is clear: it is impossible to deny successfully the validity of reason.

This, however, is not the form of Climacus' critique of reason. Reason does reveal eternal truth; to deny this is to contradict ourselves. One truth revealed by reason is the opaqueness of existence to reason. Reason, then, is absolutely valid, but is not universal in application. It proves itself incompetent to deal with existential problems.

For Climacus reason is valid – eternally so – but limited in scope. As such, it can determine that existence is closed to and cannot be penetrated by reason. Reason, then, is not rejected as such. Climacus' attack on reason cannot destroy it, but serves to reintroduce the kaleidoscopic variety of existence itself. He protests against the tendency of his time to elevate reason at the expense of other, equally important elements of existence. An increasingly scientific world remainders the elements of becoming: feeling, imagination, anxiety, and concern. The individual must return to existence without, however, giving up reason: "If thought speaks deprecatingly of the imagination, imagination in its turn speaks deprecatingly of thought; and likewise with feeling. The task is not to exalt the one at the expense of the other, but to give them an equal status, to unify them in simultaneity; the medium in which they are unified is *existence*."[2]

Man is both in time and eternal. He is in time insofar as he has feeling and imagination and suffers becoming; he is eternal because he can reason, project into the future, and reflect on his past. The task of the *Postscript* is to redress a balance realized in classic times, now lost: "I know that in Greece, at least, a thinker was not a stunted, crippled creature who produced works of art, but was himself a work of art in his existence." [3]

The *Postscript* confronts us with the passion of existence in which action, as opposed to reason, is the decisive element. Only subjectivity is adequate to meet problems of existence.

[1] Aristotle, "Metaphysics," 1006a, in W. Kaufman, *Philosophic Classics*, Englewood Cliffs, N.J., Prentice = Hall, 1961.
[2] *Postscript*, p. 311.
[3] *Postscript*, p. 269.

CHAPTER 3

SUBJECTIVITY

Man's mortality is the problem of existence which is insoluble by speculative reason; death is the subject of Climacus' concern: "I can by no means regard death as something I have understood. Before I pass over to universal history... it seems to me that I had better think about this, lest existence mock me, because I had become so learned... that I had forgotten to understand what will some time happen to me as to every human being – sometime, nay, what am I saying: suppose death were so treacherous as to come tomorrow!"[1]

And what is desired above all is personal, eternal happiness: "Now if for any individual an eternal happiness is his highest good, this will mean that all finite satisfactions are volitionally relegated to the status of what may have to be renounced in favor of an eternal happiness."[2]

The existential problem arises when we combine the certainty of *our* death with *our* fervent desire for eternal blessedness. Climacus, who wishes to secure his eternal happiness in the face of the threat of death, answers this problem in an extraordinary way. Having rejected the aid of reason, subjectivity is presented to meet this problem. A definition of subjectivity is required.

(1) Subjectivity is a passionate concern for one's being. One is subjective if and only if *his* death and *his* desire for eternal happiness is of sole concern. At every moment of living in whatever he is doing a subjective individual is absolutely interested in his eternal happiness. The subjective individual cannot absolutely be interested in both his eternal happiness, "absolute telos," *and* various relative ends. To be interested in relative ends even part of the time is to be only partly interested in the absolute end, thereby degrading that end into a rela-

---

[1] S. Kierkegaard, *Concluding Unscientific Postscript*, Princeton, N.J., Princeton University Press, 1941, pp. 148–9.

[2] *Postscript*, p. 350.

tive end: "... the absolute *telos* has the remarkable characteristic that it demands acknowledgement as the absolute *telos* every moment."[1]

No escape is possible from the threat of death; it is only delayed by frustrating acts of attempted forgetfulness. To attempt, however, to deny the threat of death by ignoring it is to forfeit the possibility of eternal happiness: "It is not entirely impossible that one who is infinitely interested in his eternal happiness may sometime come into possession of it. But it is surely quite impossible for one who has lost a sensibility for it... ever to enjoy an eternal happiness."[2]

Furthermore, the threat of non-being can sustain life by forcing us to measure every act and gesture in light of it, and by that tension keep alive the search for eternal happiness. To live less than passionately is already to have succumbed to the threat of death; there is no focus for one's actions and consequently being is dissipated. Subjectivity is keeping the threat of our death before us at all times. This is our only chance for eternal happiness.

Subjective concern, arising from the threat of death, is a quality of our inner being in which we maintain full attention on the problem of our eternal happiness rather than concentrate upon external action.

A subjective thinker will, of course, act, but these actions are insignificant in themselves, valuable only if done in relation to one's absolute *telos* or concern. *Double reflection* is acting while one is absolutely concerned with one's eternal happiness. Action is not valued for itself; it is a test, the purpose of which is to keep the threat of death in view at all times even when tempted by the distraction of action:

What serves to mark the thoroughly cultivated personality is the degree to which the thinking in which he has his daily life has a dialectical character. To have one's daily life in the decisive dialectic of the infinite, and yet continue to live: this is both the art of life and its difficulty. ... It is a well-known fact that a cannonade tends to deafen one to other sounds; but it is also a fact that persistence in enduring it may enable one to hear every word of a conversation as clearly as when all is still. Such is also the experience of one who leads an existence as spirit, intensified by reflection.[3]

No legal activities are prohibited; however, they are done with something of an absentmindedness, since the action, not prized for itself, engenders less than the highest enthusiasm. In double reflection a certain disinterestedness in the results of activities is achieved.

[1] *Postscript*, p. 359.
[2] *Postscript*, p. 20.
[3] *Postscript*, pp. 79–80.

(2) Subjectivity is truth. Subjective truth is an ethical attitude of an individual toward a doctrine. He is "edified," that is, the individual finds it to be an answer to his absolute concern. It is a *moral commitment* by the individual, not an alternative to the rational way of knowing reality. Objective truth minimizes or neglects the relationship between the individual and the truth. Objectively, one need only accept reason's conclusions; whether accepted reluctantly or joyfully is irrelevant. In subjective truth the manner of acceptance is crucial. The attitude which constitutes subjective truth is the edifying; its object is what the individual finds to be edifying *for him*, recognizing it to be the answer to his concern.[1]

Whatever a man feels to be edifying is. As long as there is something which edifies *him* and to which he relates himself absolutely, he is in subjective truth, even if he relates himself to an admitted, objective falsehood: "When the question of the truth is raised subjectively, reflection is directed subjectively to the nature of the individual's relationship; if only the mode of this relationship is in the truth, the individual is in the truth even if he should happen to be thus related to what is not true."[2]

The term "truth," then, has both an epistemological and a moral use for Climacus. Epistemologically, it is a doctrine's rational validity or invalidity. Morally, "truth" is a passionate relationship an individual has to anything he finds edifying. Climacus does not mix his modes of knowing with his moral and theological preferences; he nowhere suggests that we substitute another mode of knowing for reason. Subjectivity is not a revelation of the divine. It does not displace our knowledge of what is rationally true; it does, however, make it irrelevant. Since the quality of passion in human life is decisive and reason superfluous, subjectivity must be chosen in any conflict between subjective and objective truth: "If one who lives in the midst of Christendom goes up to the house of God... with the true conception of God in his knowledge, and prays, but prays in a false spirit; and one who lives in an idolatrous community prays with the entire passion of the infinite, although his eyes rest upon the image of an idol: where is there most truth? The one prays in truth to God though he worships an idol; the other prays falsely to the true God, and hence worships in fact an idol."[3]

---

[1] *Postscript*, p. 226.
[2] *Postscript*, p. 178.
[3] *Postscript*, pp. 179

(3) Subjectivity is freedom. In subjectivity there can be no legislation of one will to another. The individual in his subjectivity is radically alone. An individual "a" is not subjective if another "b" attempts to be subjective for him, even if "b" is absolutely concerned about "a's" eternal happiness. An individual is subjective only if it is *he* who is concerned about his own eternal happiness. But, then, it is necessary to explain why there is no loss of subjectivity in accepting Climacus' doctrine of subjectivity. Is this not subjecting our will to another?

For Climacus subjectivity does not demand the absence of all external causes or influences. Subjectivity is satisfied with whatever or whomever causes the individual to have concern. Climacus himself attempts to be a cause of increased subjectivity in the individual; he instructs, edifies, and preaches. He offers what he considers the limits of help one man can give another in his subjectivity: "The very maximum of what one human being can do for another in relation to that wherein each man has to do solely with himself, is to inspire him with concern and unrest."[1] And, within those limits, he attempts to inspire that concern and unrest.

In the *Postscript* help through indirect communication reaches its height. After continually affirming that subjectivity is truth, Climacus now denies it: "Subjectivity, inwardness, has been posited as the truth; can any expression for the truth be found which has a still higher degree of inwardness? Aye, there is such an expression, provided the principle that subjectivity or inwardness is the truth begins by positing the opposite principle: that subjectivity is untruth."[2]

Here it is necessary to distinguish the path of a movement from its content, that is, *how* a doctrine is asserted as against *what* is said. To talk about the truth of subjectivity and then to deny its truth is to create in us the possibility of just such a movement to subjectivity. By confronting us with paradox we are frustrated and thus may be forced back to ourselves and our concern. Climacus' nullification of assertions continually made by him is the last term in an ironic yet humane dialectic. This does not bring us back to the innocent beginning but rather to a new level of confrontation.

Climacus, then, attempts to influence our subjectivity. Nonetheless, for all the help offered by him, the individual in subjectivity is alone; it is *he* who must be concerned, and about *his* welfare. This concern

---

[1] *Postscript*, p. 346.
[2] *Postscript*, p. 185.

separates him absolutely from every other individual who must exhibit concern for himself. The concern of another can be the occasion for the individual himself becoming concerned about himself. For example, a teacher presenting an individual with a challenge, in this case, the exhortation to become subjective, *and*, alternately, the demand not to become subjective, may help cause a reaction in an individual resulting in his subjectivity. The teacher's task is to repel and frustrate *in a way* that drives the individual into himself. Socratic help is the model.

That one is concerned and not merely mouthing the concern of others is not easily discovered; there are indications, however, of our condition.

How can we determine another's subjectivity? (a) The question, although meaningless, suggests an important problem involving the determination of our own subjectivity. (b)There are signs accompanying subjectivity or the lack of it; these signs are only clues, not logical demonstrations.

(a) The investigation of another's subjectivity is important only if it gives an individual insight into his own condition. By observing patterns in another that he himself may possess the individual may be helped to a greater understanding of himself. To investigate another's subjectivity in order to expose that person is only to reveal one's lack of subjectivity, for it is to engage in a task irrelevant to subjective concern.

An important problem, then, is the determination of the true state of our own subjectivity. Are there clues to our own subjectivity or lack of it?

(b) Signs of subjectivity appear in the life pattern of an individual. To discover this requires looking at actions as well as assertions, the nuances of an assertion as well as its literal content, and, finally, omissions as well as specifications of assertion: ". . . when a man speaks about death, and of how he has... conceived its uncertainty... it does not follow that he has really done it. But there is a more artistic way of finding out whether he lies or not. Merely let him speak: if he is a deceiver, he will contradict himself precisely when he is... offering the most solemn assurances. The contradiction. . . consists in the failure of the speech to include a consciousness of what the speech professes directly to assert."[1]

Certain signs indicating a lack of subjectivity suggest themselves

[1] *Postscript*, pp. 151–2.

immediately. For example, it is clear that subjectivity cannot allow a fraternity of subjectivists to gain their inspiration from shared experiences. In subjectivity a man has to do with himself, and here brotherhood may be a sign of a lack of subjectivity.

This is also true of any position which draws attention to and invites admiration of one's subjectivity. Thus, for example, the life of the cloister. By symbolizing subjectivity, by giving outward testimony, and bestowing official symbols of office upon it, subjectivity is endangered: "The cloister wishes to express inwardness by means of a specific outwardness which is supposed to be inwardness. But this is a contradiction, for being a monk is just as truly something external as being an alderman."[1]

Another sign of a lack of subjectivity is given by those who make a living from subjectivity. To cry "despair" is to externalize what must be an internal matter; if it is truly important, it must remain the subject of a dialogue between the individual and himself. If not, the suspicion is that subjectivity is being commercialized.

Signs, however, are not necessary indicators of the true state of the human being. The dialogue of the spirit with itself or with another can be infinitely subtle. The spirit may offer signs indicating a lack of subjectivity but in the service of that subjectivity. A truly subjective person may keep his subjectivity intact by making a double movement: proclaiming his subjectivity publicly but in an unbelievable way. By his profession of subjectivity, the truly subjective individual is saved from his critics. They no longer believe he possesses subjectivity and condemn him to the realm of the uninteresting. Conversely, the movement away from subjectivity can utilize many of the conventional symbols for subjectivity. The suffering unto despair which would seem to be the surest sign of subjectivity may be done for the joy of suffering, and, if so, is the very antithesis of subjectivity even when consistently and piously exhibited. In the world of the spirit a sign's meaning can be infinitely rich or ambiguous. *Double movement* arises when signs can be created to anticipate responses in an observer rather than simply standing for an inner state. When this possibility appears the attempt to understand another or even oneself by signs is jeopardized. We may present both to ourselves and others signs which are either indicators or masks of our true condition. Accuracy in the interpretation of signs depends upon the sensitivity of the observer in perceiving the unguarded movement of himself and others.

[1] *Postscript*, p. 366.

Even when, however, double movement appears in an individual, further understanding of one's own subjectivity may be gained by observing our generalizations and judgments of that double movement and its complex possibilities. Although an ambiguous sign may yield no one necessarily correct interpretation, one's subjectivity or lack of it may be significantly revealed by his particular interpretation of that ambiguous sign. As Kierkegaard says: "... all doubly reflected communication makes contrary interpretation equally possible, and the judge will be made manifest by his judgment."[1] However, the reading of ambiguous signs is itself susceptible to double movement, thereby infinitely complicating the understanding of signs.

There are, then, signs of subjectivity and the lack of it. As soon as the possibility of double movement arises, however, signs of subjectivity become ambiguous; they are only clues; accuracy of interpretation depends upon the sense and sensibility of the person viewing them.

(4) Subjectivity is suffering. The cause of suffering is the awareness of the totality of our guilt. Guilt is entailed by a dialectic having the following movement: First, there is a desire to be subjective. Second, there is the realization of the demands of true subjectivity. Finally, in aspiring to realize ourselves at every moment we are conscious of our failure to attain complete subjectivity. This failure is our guilt.

Guilt is the awareness of the disproportion between the attempt to be subjective and the requirements of true subjectivity. The effect of guilt is suffering. We suffer when we realize our part in the failure to exist inwardly; we blame ourselves for our failure to attain complete subjectivity.

The lack of proportion between our striving and our attainment of absolute inwardness is explained in the following way: First, there are practical difficulties in realizing subjectivity at every moment. To be seriously concerned about our eternal happiness only some of the time is to have a relative relationship to the absolute concern. Subjectivity demands all of our being for all our lifetime; there can be no shortcuts. Ordinarily we reward someone who completes his work before the allotted time; now the task is to be subjective for all of the time that is given to us. We know what is required; yet fail to do it at every moment. The realization of our failure causes our suffering.

Second, even the decision to be subjective throws one immediately

<hr>

[1] S. Kierkegaard, *The Point of View for My Work as An Author: A Report to History*, New York, Harper & Brothers, p. 156.

into guilt. To deliberate about becoming subjective is not yet to be subjective: "... even at the instant when the task is clearly set there has been some waste for meanwhile time has passed, and the beginning was not made at once... it is discovered that there, since time has meanwhile been passing, an ill beginning is made, and that the beginning must be made by becoming guilty and from that moment increasing the total capital guilt by a new guilt at a usurious rate of interest."[1]

Finally, the number of failures in realizing subjectivity is not decisive; quality, not quantity, determines guilt; that we have only once failed to attain subjectivity is crucial; it is enough to throw us into total, infinite guilt. The individual is responsible for all of himself; he offers himself wholly in the search for eternal happiness. We can never forget the guilt we have contracted in our search for eternal happiness. The child can wipe away uncomfortable memories, always beginning anew; the individual in attempting to relate his whole being to eternal happiness must carry with him the memory of his guilt. One guilt is infinite and total; the necessity of our recollection of it is our punishment.

To recapitulate: the suffering of the subjective individual is entailed by the fact that he carries with him at all times in his search for eternal happiness the awareness of the disproportion he has created between his existence and the demands of subjectivity. This is the pathos of the existing individual and his guilt. But it is only in desiring to be subjective that he has taken on the burden of guilt consciousness and therefore suffers. Without the attempt to be subjective there can be no guilt, for there is no disproportion between desire and command. Therefore the objective man is without guilt, being without subjectivity. Conversely, the more subjective the individual is, the greater the realization there is of the disproportion between desire and demand, that is, the more he feels his guilt and must suffer. The suffering produced in the truly subjective individual creates a despair in living at all. Suicide would, however, remove him from subjectivity and his possibility for eternal happiness. Guilt and suffering to the point of suicide is the fate of the truly aspiring but imperfectly subjective individual: "Just because the existential pathos is not an affair of the moment but demands persistence, the exister himself... will seek to discover the minimum of forgetfulness which is required for holding

1 *Postscript*, P. 469.

out, since he himself is aware that the instantaneous is a misapprehension."[1] Subjectivity then is suffering.

In conclusion, subjectivity is (1) a passionate concern for one's being, which is threatened by death, relating oneself at all times to this concern; (2) it demands an adherence to anything which the individual finds edifying; (3) it entails an isolation in freedom and an uncertainty of even possessing subjectivity; (4) finally, it is a suffering which is masked from the world.

There is only one in whom subjective concern can be met truly: Jesus Christ.

---

[1] *Postscript*, pp. 477-78.

CHAPTER 4

THE PARADOX

Man's quest for eternal happiness, his salvation and freedom from death, is met by Christianity. To be a Christian is to accept the Paradox of Jesus as Christ, man as God: "The characteristic mark of Christianity is the paradox, the absolute paradox."[1]

God, infinite, omniscient, and omnipotent, nevertheless came into time born of woman, grew, and died. Jesus Christ is, at every moment, omniscient; yet, as befits man, He is limited in intelligence, omnipotent yet weak, benevolent yet capable of evil. As Anselm says: "... if these two complete natures are said to be joined somehow, in such a way that one may be Divine while the other is human, and yet that which is God not be the same with that which is man, it is impossible for both to do the work necessary to be accomplished. For God will not do it, because he has no debt to pay; and man will not do it, because he cannot. Therefore... it is necessary that the same being should be perfect God and perfect man..."[2]

Christianity presents many difficulties to the rational mind. Its specific offense against reason, however, is its concept of the coming into time of the Eternal solely to suffer. This Paradox is the ultimate challenge to the intellect, for all attempts to understand it must conform to the laws of judgment and discourse: identity, contradiction, and excluded middle. Yet the Paradox violates these laws. To say that at the same time and in the same respect one is and is not finite is to speak nonsense, or, worse, it is madness. Rationally, the statement "God-man" is a nonsensical statement.

Therefore any justification for the acceptance of Jesus Christ must

[1] S. Kierkegaard, *Concluding Unscientific Postscript*, Princeton, N.J., Princeton University Press, 1941, p. 480.

[2] St. Anselm, *Proslogium; Monologium, An Appendix in Behalf of the Fool by Gaunilon; and Cur Deus Homo*, La Salle, Ill. 5, Open Court Publishing Company, 1951, pp. 245-6.

be examined. In brief: there are no reasons for accepting the Paradox. If any could be found the Paradox would be a rational answer to our problem of eternal happiness, encountering the same objections put forth by Climacus in his critique of reason.

Therefore believing in the Paradox the Christian is a fool: "Christianity has declared itself to be the eternal essential truth which has come into being in time. It has proclaimed itself as the *Paradox*, and it has required of the individual the inwardness of faith in relation to that which stamps itself as an offense to the Jews and a folly to the Greeks – and an absurdity to the understanding."[1]

His folly is plural: (1) The Christian supposes that Jesus as Christ existed. This assumption violates reason. First, it goes against the highest standards of historical evidence, sense-experience, and scientific knowledge. Furthermore, the supposition is weakened by the imperiousness of its claim; Christianity asserts its belief in the existence of the God-man absolutely; it cannot be satisfied with evidence which might establish a possibility in its behalf. But reason can offer only approximation. Finally, it is a rationally impossible position. Climacus' demonstration of reason as approximate is itself a rational critique; as such it claims to be valid rationally. Any critique of reason by reason leaves always a valid residue of reason, for any attempt to deny rationally the validity of reason uses reason. A rational critique of reason can only indicate limits in the range of reason's use; it cannot deny reason's validity. This residue of reason is the laws of identity, contradiction, and excluded middle, laws whose denial, as Aristotle said, is impossible: "Evidently then such a principle is the most certain of all... It is, that the same attribute cannot at the same time belong and not belong to the same subject and in the same respect... This, then, is the most certain of all principles, since it answers to the definition given above. For it is impossible for any one to believe the same thing to be and not to be, as some think Heraclitus says."[2] Climacus, using these absolute laws in criticizing reason's attempt to go beyond its proper limits, admits their validity. Yet the Paradox, stating that something is both man and not-man (God) at the same time and in the same respect, violates these laws; thus the Paradox denies reason, one in faith being irrational or mad.

(2) The Paradox violates common sense. Once we accept the Paradox

---

[1] *Postscript*, p. 191.
[2] Aristotle, "Metaphysics" in *The Basic Works of Aristotle*, New York, Random House, 1941, pp. 736–7.

the sacrifice of prudent standards is possible – if the God of faith commands. In the history of revelation almost everything, no matter how bizarre and impractical, has been interpreted as God's command to the faithful. By recognizing only those revelations in harmony with Scripture, Christianity has prevented a chaos of revelatory commands. As H. Richard Niebuhr says: "Can we not say that when we speak of God and revelation we mean events which occur in the privacy of our personal, inner life or what we feel to be basic in our moral consciousness? Yet once more we discover that visions... may be interpreted in many ways. The "true" seed within, the "right" spirit, can be distinguished from false seeds and evil spirits only by the use of criteria which are not purely individual and biographical."[1] The vision of the daemonic is rejected, barred by both Scripture and tradition. Climacus, however, lacks these restraints; it is impossible to authenticate Scripture or verify traditions; interpretation of its meaning can only be speculative.

Since for Climacus Scripture and tradition cannot be an ultimate standard in determining what is proper revelation, anything is acceptable. Common sense has no secure control on the Christian's action, having itself no stable guide in Scripture.

(3) The Paradox may entail the usurpation of the ethical. In subjectivity the individual is prohibited from doing anything illegal; in faith the Paradox may demand a break with the ethical, with universal standards of decent and human conduct: "Duty is the absolute, its requirement an absolute requirement, and yet the individual is prevented from realizing it... in a desperate ironical manner he is as if set free..."[2] This rupture may be a lawless, immoral act that makes the striving after the Paradox insane; it is a madness which may even take the form of a willingness to "sacrifice," that is, murder.[3]

(4) In accepting the Paradox we recognize that we are sinners, know we are not the cause, and yet realize we must suffer because we are in sin: "From eternity the individual is not a sinner; so when the being who is planned on the scale of eternity comes into the world by birth, he becomes a sinner at birth or is born a sinner..."[4]

In believing, we realize our sin – defined as our being parted from God – and must take on the burden of the consciousness of our sepa-

---

[1] H. Richard Neibuhr, *The Meaning of Revelation*, New York, The Macmillan Company, 1941, p. 52.
[2] *Postscript*, p. 239.
[3] *Postscript*, pp. 238–9.
[4] *Postscript*, p. 517.

ration from God. Yet it is madness to suffer sin because in being born we are not responsible for having severed our God-relationship.

(5) The suffering the faithful endure is intensified by the knowledge that they can never know whether they are in faith, since signs indicating faith are always ambiguous. The impossibility of knowing our condition adds another measure of folly to that of being a Christian. Since signs of faith are ambiguous, any act relating to belief is infected by the possibility that the command to act, rather than coming from God, may be psychologically motivated. The certainty of command afforded by the paradigm case of temptation and revelation in the Bible, the trial of Abraham, is not given to ordinary mortals: "The awakened person knows himself to be absolutely secure in his own God-relationship ... this security is unfortunately the one certain sign that the individual does not stand in a relationship to God..."[1]

(6) Finally, the acceptance of the Paradox destroys man's proper self-esteem. Before God the individual is totally helpless; he is nothing; the individual is destroyed by Christianity: "Even though it be true that the conception of God is the absolute help, it is also the only help which is absolutely capable of revealing to man his own helplessness."[2]

The true Christian is a fool possessed by the daemonic, a lover of suffering, one who rejects the absolute reign of reasonable ethical standards erected by decent men, a fanatic who would destroy the self, leaving him helpless before an Absurd Being who can in no sane way be certified as existing. This is the price paid by those who have an *expectation* of an eternal happiness, whose only certain sign seems to be a perverse finding of happiness in suffering: "... let us return to suffering as the sign of happiness."[3]

Reason and sanity deny Christianity, and therefore must be rejected by Christianity. True faith demands that the Christian believe in the Paradox despite *objective certainty that the doctrine of God-man is false.* We can know rationally that the Paradox can never be: "When Socrates believed that there was a God, he held fast to the objective uncertainty with the whole passion of his inwardness... Now it is otherwise. Instead of the objective uncertainty, there is here a certainty, namely, that objectively it is absurd; and this absurdity, held fast in the passion of inwardness, is faith."[4]

[1] *Postscript*, p. 406.
[2] *Postscript*, p. 433.
[3] *Postscript*, p. 408.
[4] *Postscript*, p. 188.

In conclusion, for Climacus, man's quest for eternal happiness is to be met only by Christianity. To be a Christian is to accept the Paradox of Jesus as Christ. Yet to make this acceptance is to sacrifice our reason and doing so, as Climacus shows, is the most difficult task of all.

Climacus' faith opposes all popular notions of faith. For example, William James states that, [1] in the absence of full knowledge, it is intelligent to believe. When there is insufficient evidence to decide the issue, the courageous will postulate concepts that cannot be verified but are necessary to affirm life in the midst of objective uncertainty. Socrates had faith; despite objective uncertainty, that is, a lack of complete rational evidence, he supposed a concept of God. But for Climacus this is paganism; it is not a Christianity that is offered *against* good and sufficient knowledge of the *impossibility* of the Paradox – "an offence to the Jews and folly to the Greeks." The Paradox demands belief in spite of the intellect, not speculation in the absence of understanding: "It [Christianity] requires that the individual should existentially venture all... This is something that a pagan can also do; he may, for example, venture everything on an immortality's perhaps. But Christianity also requires that the individual risk his thought, venturing to believe against the understanding..."[2]

The movement to faith, then, involves the following steps: (i) A realization that the Paradox is absurd, that is, it violates reason, and that to reject rational standards of judgment is to allow the daemonic. (ii) Realizing the rational impossibility of the Paradox one nevertheless believes *against* his reason. The Christian supposes Jesus Christ to give him eternal happiness although he knows the claim to be without justification. Christianity rejects the dictates of reason while realizing them to be the standard of truth and sanity in this world. To be in faith means that one expects the impossible while realizing the expectation to be mad. The naive believer, unaware of the difficulties of believing, that is, not believing *in spite of* the knowledge of its madness, is not in faith: "Christianity has helped men to a vision of it – by means of the absurd. When this last qualification is omitted, everything has indeed become much easier than it was in paganism. But if the point is held fast, everything is far more difficult..."[3]

There can, then, be no reconciliation of Christianity and reason.

---

[1] William James, *The Will to Believe*, New York, Longmans, Green, and Co., 1911, p. 26.
[2] *Postscript*, p. 384.
[3] *Postscript*, p. 384.

Rationalizing Christianity has corrupted it. The Christian claim is foolish; to affirm this absurdity knowing it to be such is to be a Christian.

APPENDIX

I have interpreted reason and faith to be in opposition in the *Postscript*. There is an alternative interpretation. A tradition in Kierkegaardian scholarship denies any real conflict between faith and reason. Reason tells us nothing about the truth of the Paradox. Faith or belief in the Paradox is *above*, not against, reason, *supra rationem*, not *contra rationem*. These positions, "above" or "against," are represented in traditional theological thought by Tertullian and St. Thomas. As attributed to Tertullian: *Credo quia absurdum est*, believe because it is impossible. Faith stands opposed to reason. To be in faith one must deny reason. For Thomas reason and faith do not conflict. That God is, can be known through reason. To know what God is, reason must be led by faith and revelation but discovers nothing that contradicts reason.

Climacus accepts neither the Tertullian nor the Thomistic positions. I shall demonstrate the following conclusion regarding Climacus' position. The relation of faith to reason for Climacus is neither that of "above" nor "against" but rather of both. By reason "against" faith is meant that faith contradicts the laws of reason, and therefore one must choose to be rational or in faith. Either/Or. By faith "above" reason is meant that reason cannot pass judgments upon the reality or existence of the object of faith. Climacus' answer is that reason is "against" faith in the sense that reason finds faith to violate standards of proper reason, contradicting the laws of logic. Faith, then, can never be in harmony with reason. This is to deny the Thomistic interpretation. I will also show that Climacus maintains faith is "above" reason in the sense that reason and faith do not conflict on the existential level. This interpretation denies Tertullian's position. Climacus offers a new answer to the problem of the relation of faith to reason.

To demonstrate this I examine the tradition that finds in Climacus no essential conflict between faith and reason. Having expounded those

passages in the *Postscript* which seem quite clearly to indicate a conflict between faith and reason, I will now examine the position of
Professor N. H. Søe, who argues for the harmony of reason and faith
in his essay "Kierkegaard's Doctrine of the Paradox" in *A Kierkegaard
Critique*.

I will then show how Climacus' stand consistently transcends both
Tertullian's position of faith against reason and the Thomistic one of
faith above reason.

Six arguments are given by Professor Søe to prove that there is no
basic conflict between faith and reason.

(1) Søe offers text which would seem to substantiate the position
that reason is against faith. The absurd acceptance of the Paradox of
Jesus Christ engenders the conflict between reason and faith. But,
despite appearances, the Paradox is not in conflict with the intellect.
The Paradox of the God-man is a *doctrine*, that is, the Athanasian
creed of the God-man decided in church council at Chalcedon and,
since Climacus denies doctrine as existentially useless, he must then
deny the importance of the doctrine of the God-man. Thus there is no
shock to the understanding; faith presents nothing paradoxical or
contradictory to the understanding. Climacus is concerned with existential, not doctrinal, affairs; there is no conflict between reason and
faith. Søe says:

> This might be thought proof that Kierkegaard really finds the shock to the
> understanding to be caused by a definite paradoxical doctrine, namely, "the
> Athanasian two-nature doctrine" as Bohlin calls it (p. 173) and as N. Teisen
> had maintained as early as 1903. However, it will at once be noticed that
> Kierkegaard himself expressly and emphatically protested against this inter-
> pretation. Anti-Climacus states that "Christianity is not a doctrine. All talk
> about offense in relation to Christianity as a doctrine is a misunderstanding,
> it is a device to mitigate the shock of the offense at the scandal –, as, for example,
> when one speaks of the offense of the *doctrine* of the God-man and the *doctrine*
> of the Atonement. No, the offense is related either to Christ or to the fact of
> being oneself a Christian".[1]

Reply: Søe calls the Paradox a doctrine. He then implies that since
Climacus denies doctrines he must deny the doctrine of the Paradox.
Climacus, however, does not call the Paradox a doctrine; it is not.

Furthermore, to deny the conflict between reason and faith, removing the Absurd by labeling it a doctrine and therefore not crucial,
is to misunderstand the notion of "doctrine." "Doctrine" has the

---

[1] Howard Johnson, Niels Thulstrup, editors, *A Kierkegaard Critique*, New York, Harper &
Row, 1962, pp. 210–11.

meaning of a content objectively asserted. Existential communication, on the contrary, is content that is subjectively appropriated: "... it is one thing for something to be a philosophical doctrine which desires to be intellectually grasped and speculatively understood, and quite another thing to be a doctrine that proposes to be realized in existence... in connection with a doctrine of the latter sort... the task is to exist in it, in understanding the difficulty of existing in it, and what a tremendous existential task such a doctrine posits for the learner."[1]

The difference between doctrine and existential communication is not that a doctrine has a content or message and existential communication does not, but that existential communication is a personal appropriation of a content whereas doctrine is not. There can be no assertions without content; this is an absurdity. To assert a supposedly meaningless proposition is to make at least one meaningful assertion about it, namely, that the statement is meaningless. The meaning that a meaningless proposition carries is the assertion that one can afford to ignore it since it says nothing. Climacus makes assertions; he formulates propositions; his statements have content. "Doctrine" is to be avoided, not because it contains an assertion such as the Athanasian code, but because it asserts the Athanasian code *objectively*, that is, without personal appropriation. The Athanasian code is not a doctrine if it is appropriated by an individual who is concerned. Thus Climacus does not call the Paradox a doctrine, and does not use the Paradox as a doctrine. It is used continuously by him as a supreme irritant, challenging us to confront true Christianity.

(2) The Absolute Paradox and its shock to the understanding is only a subsidiary problem for Climacus. It is Lessing's doctrine that salvation or eternal blessedness is to be gained by something presenting itself in time that provides the real problem of the *Postscript*. Thus the Paradox and the offense it presents to reason must be understood as peripheral. Søe states:

It is, however, of decisive importance for an understanding of the whole problem to realize that when Kierkegaard, particularly in the Climacus works, gives special attention to the Incarnation of the God-Man as if this were of the greatest importance, it is not due to a particular predilection for an "Athanasian two-nature doctrine" and the "shock" this apparently gives the understanding. If one has such an impression, then the whole purpose of these works has been misunderstood. What is most important for Climacus is the problem raised by Lessing of eternal salvation being dependent upon something historical, of

---

[1] *Postscript*, p. 339.

eternity being encountered in a decisive way in a fact which, since it is historical, must appear relative, fortuitous, and merely "temporal."[1]

Reply: This argument does not deny that the Paradox is an offense to the understanding. It suggests only that the Paradox is not crucial, and then argues for a concentration upon the central problem of the *Postscript*: Lessing's statement that blessedness is decided in time through the relationship to "something historical." This "something historical," however, cannot be any historical item. Blessedness is gained only by relating oneself to a particular "something historical" which is, of course, the Paradox of Jesus-Christ, the eternal in time: "... the existing individual does not in the course of time come into relation with the eternal and think about it (this is A), but *in time* it comes into relation with the eternal *in time*..."[2]

Lessing's statement does not obviate the crucial position of the Paradox as an offense to reason; it requires it. One is confronted with the Paradox, that "something historical," which is the only hope for salvation; it is the difficulty, if not impossibility, of relating oneself to an absurdity that makes Christianity the most desperate exercise of will and Lessing's problem meaningful.

(3) The Paradox is not an offense against reason; it offends man's heart. As Søe says:

> Another extremely important point can be expressed in a slightly different way: in *Philosophical Fragments* it is asserted that the Incarnation "is a folly to the understanding and an offense to the human heart." Here the offense caused by the Paradox is not seen in relation to the mind but to the heart. Kierkegaard (Climacus) does not elaborate this further. That this remark should occur in this particular work is astonishing and therefore worthy of attention. It indicates, undoubtedly, Kierkegaard's awareness of the fact that the Incarnation, as he understands it, does cause "offense" as it wounds human self-confidence. It offends man by revealing that he "is in untruth" owing to his very nature. Basically, it is not the understanding which is compromised; the offense goes deeper, it cuts to the heart.[3]

Reply: In *Philosophical Fragments* the term "offense" describes the shock of the Paradox to the heart, not the head. In the *Postscript* Climacus uses the term "offense" to describe the shock of the Paradox to the head, not to the heart: "But the paradox, which requires faith against the understanding, at once brings to evidence the offense..."[4]

It is irrelevant that the term "offense" as used in the *Philosophical*

1 *Critique*, p. 214.
2 *Postscript*, p. 506.
3 *Critique*, p. 216.
4 *Postscript*, p. 518.

Fragments does not denote the opposition of faith to reason. The term is used to denote such opposition by Climacus in the *Postscript*.

Furthermore, finding that the term "offense" is not used in the *Fragments* to denote the opposition of faith to reason does not thereby lessen that offense. Whether the term "offense" or "folly" is used to denote reason's judgment of faith, the opposition of faith to reason is not removed by citing the uses of the term "offense."

Finally, Climacus states that the Paradox offends the heart as well as the head. But this offense *follows* from the offense to the understanding (see p. 30). In denying reason the Paradox may violate ethical standards which are a function of reason and whose violation offers the severest offense to the heart of man. Ethics which is universal imposes obligations upon all men. Ethics is duty which commands the universal over the individual, the abstract over the concrete, the whole above the part. It wills that we refuse to make ourselves the exception and that we obey law which is applied to all equally. To reject reason for faith allows the irrational and the unethical: the holding of the individual above the whole, the putting of one's own interest above that of the group. It is the denial of the command of reason and the universal obligation to obey it, resulting in fearful consequences as in Abraham's case when failing to do so, that causes the severest offense to the heart. Faith frees one from reason and its effects: the rule by law over all men. The consequence of irrationality may be immorality.

There are many offenses committed by Christianity; the offense to the heart follows from the shock to the understanding and the rejection of reason. Søe's argument broadens the scandal of Christianity; it does not remove the conflict between reason and faith.

(4) Faith is not anti-rational; it is non-rational. Reason does not prove the impossibility or absurdity of faith; we can know only that reason cannot prove necessary the rational truth of the Paradox. Søe's argument is:

When he [Climacus] states repeatedly . . . that the important thing is "to understand that faith cannot be understood," this has nothing to do with "irrational practical experience" as opposed to clear thinking. It is merely the way in which the honest thinker expresses his recognition of the fact that the content of religious doctrines cannot be proved *necessary*, in the manner of a Hegel or a Martensen, from one or another given premise, and that, for this reason, there cannot be a Christian dogmatic system. It is not possible, for example, to deduce from one or another recognized fact the necessity of the Incarnation. This does not mean that we are faced with irrational practical experience; we are faced, rather, with a message, something which comes from outside, a revealed proclamation, the logical necessity of which can never be understood by us even though, as Kierkegaard remarks half ironically. . . it may be understood by God him-self.[1]

Reply: There are two forms of faith for Climacus. The first risks everything on an uncertainty; it ventures to believe in something that may possibly be true rationally but for which there is not sufficient evidence to decide: "An objective uncertainty held fast in an appropri-ation-process of the most passionate inwardness is the truth, the highest truth attainable for an existing individual. But the above definition of truth is an equivalent expression for faith. Without risk there is no faith. Faith is precisely the contradiction between the infinite pas-sion of the individual's inwardness and the objective uncertainty."[2]

The second or Christian faith is to risk everything on a certainty, namely, that what is believed is known to be absurd, rationally im-possible. Reason necessarily finds the Christian Paradox to violate the truth of reason: "When Socrates believed that there was a God, he held fast to the objective uncertainty with the whole passion of his inwardness, and it is precisely in this contradiction and in this risk, that faith is rooted. Now it is otherwise. Instead of the objective un-certainty, there is here a certainty, namely, that objectively it is ab-surd; and this absurdity, held fast in the passion of inwardness, is faith."[3]

Christian faith is, then, proven necessary by reason; it is proven to be a certain rational impossibility. To attempt to show that reason cannot with certainty disprove faith is to lapse into non-Christian faith: "With the help of the approximation-process the absurd be-comes... probable... Anything that is almost probable... is some-thing he [a man who wishes to acquire faith] can almost know... but it is impossible to *believe*. For the absurd is the object of faith, and the only object that can be believed."[4]

Furthermore, as Søe indicates, Climacus says that the Paradox can-not be understood. This, says Søe, is because the Paradox is *beyond* understanding; to say something cannot be understood means not that it is not true, but that we cannot determine whether it is. But there is another equally plausible interpretation of the statement that the Paradox cannot be understood. If something is an absurdity, it is not understandable. Common meanings of "understand" are to know something, to discern its rational pattern, or to render experience in-

[1] *Critique*, p. 218.
[2] *Postscript*, p. 182.
[3] *Postscript*, p. 188.
[4] *Postscript*, p. 189.

telligible. Since the Paradox is not rational it is, in this sense, not understandable. By this interpretation of the statement "the Paradox cannot be understood," meaning thereby that the Paradox is irrational, the opposition of reason and faith is made clear. I do not offer this interpretation as necessary. I do maintain, however, that the phrase, "the Paradox cannot be understood," is no evidence of the truth of the thesis that faith is beyond reason, not against it.

Finally, Søe notes Climacus' remark that the Paradox may be the truth for God. Again, this is ambiguous. Truth has several meanings for Climacus, including a moral use: to be true means to be appropriated by an individual. To say that the Paradox is true for God need mean only that God is the Paradox. However, the Paradox may be true rationally for God, since God is the Paradox, and from the Paradox anything is possible. Reason, however, as our standard, proves faith a rational absurdity.

There is, then, no textual warrant for saying that the only opposition between faith and reason is that reason cannot prove necessary the truth of faith. Reason, says Climacus, proves necessary the absurdity of faith, and only this is Christian faith.

(5) In the *Journals* Kierkegaard denies that the Paradox is self-contradictory. Therefore, there is no conflict between faith and reason since the Paradox does not violate any rules of reason. Søe says: "Kierkegaard asserts plainly and objectively that there is 'no self-contradiction' in the idea that 'Christ was God in the guise of a servant.'..."[1]

Reply: A Paradox is, by definition, contradictory. Climacus does not deny this; he asserts the contradiction of the Christian Paradox in the *Postscript*: "... there are two dialectical contradictions, first, the basing of one's eternal happiness upon the relation to something historical, and then the fact that this historical datum is compounded in a way contradictory to all thinking..."[1]

The most that could be established by Søe's text is not that there is no opposition between faith and reason but that Kierkegaard is inconsistent, in the *Postscript* calling the Paradox a contradiction, in the *Journals* a non-contradiction. Kierkegaard, however, is not inconsistent. Søe finds one passage which seems to deny the analytic truth that the Paradox is a paradox, that is, is self-contradictory. This passage, however, does not support his position. Kierkegaard says

[1] *Critique*, p. 219.
[2] *Postscript*, p. 513.

there is no contradiction in the statement that Christ was God in the guise of a servant. And there is none – since this is not the statement of the Paradox. The Paradox is that Jesus *is* Christ, not that Christ was God *in the guise of* a servant. "In the guise of" removes the contradiction from the Absolute Paradox. The union of absolutely incompatible elements, man and God, is denied by saying that God was in the guise of (but not really) man. "In the guise of" removes that incompatibility, enabling us to deny the forced union of two separate and contrary elements by giving the human half of the God-man Paradox less than full ontological status. To treat this statement as the Paradox would allow us to explain away the difficulties of the Paradox, making Christianity easier but also willing its destruction.

(6) There are two meanings of "absurd." Climacus characterizes the Christian Paradox as absurd in a way that is to be distinguished from the absurd which is mere nonsense. Since Climacus rejects nonsense whose essence is self-contradiction and therefore against reason, there is no conflict between reason and the absurdity of the Paradox which, since it is not nonsense, is not self-contradictory. Thus Climacus is talking very loosely when he refers to the opposition of faith and reason in relation to the true Paradox. Those who set the Absurd Paradox as being against reason by being contradictory do not distinguish between the true Absurd and mere nonsense. Søe presents this argument:

> In actual fact, however, this is made clear in the numerous pronouncements delivered by Kierkegaard and his pseudonyms to prevent the misunderstanding that "the absurd" as the object of faith is the same as "the absurd in the vulgar sense of the word." As early a work as the *Philosophical Fragments* it is expressly stated that the mind can examine the fact of the Incarnation ("the Deity in time") and "the individual's particular relationship to the Deity." Something quite different must be said in the case of the meaningless, for that is not only "an absurdity," like the genuine paradox, but also "contains a self-contradiction." The latter (in this connection it is the idea that a man could generate faith in another man and so become "God" for him) is pure "twaddle" and therefore lies on an entirely different plane from the paradox of faith. Similarly, it is asserted in the *Postscript* that there is something which must be described as "nonsense," and no man can believe this "against the understanding," for precisely the understanding will discern that it is nonsense and will prevent him from believing it; but he makes so much use of the understanding that he becomes aware of the incomprehensible and then he holds to this, believing against the understanding.
>
> Climacus is therefore talking very loosely when he says that the paradox wills "the downfall of reason" or that "the paradoxical passion of reason," "without rightly understanding itself," "is bent upon its own downfall" or that "reason yielded itself" or "sets itself aside." If this were taken in the radical sense insisted upon by some scholars, it would be impossible to distinguish

between the meaningful paradox of faith and that which is nonsensical or absurd in the vulgar sense of the word.[1]

I understand Søe's argument to have the following form: (1) There are two meanings of absurd. (2) One meaning of absurd is that which contains a self-contradiction. This will be called "nonsense" or absurdity in the vulgar sense of the term. (3) There is another absurd. No defining characteristic of it is given by Søe except that it is other than nonsense. This will be called the "true absurd." (4) Climacus rejects the vulgar use of absurdity or nonsense as applying to the Paradox. (5) What remains then is the true absurd which does apply to the Paradox; it is not self-contradictory since the essence of nonsense is self-contradiction and the true absurd is other than nonsense, therefore other than self-contradictory. There is, then, no conflict between the Christian faith which is the true absurd and reason since the Paradox which is the true absurd is not self-contradictory.

Reply: Climacus does distinguish two meanings of absurd: the vulgar meaning of absurd or "nonsense" and the true absurd of the Paradox, called the "Incomprehensible." However it is (1) *inaccurate* to say that the criterion of nonsense is self-contradiction in the logical sense and (2) a *non sequitur* to say that, because nonsense is self-contradictory (which it is not), the true absurd or Incomprehensible is therefore *not* self-contradictory (which it is).

(1) The "self-contradiction" that characterizes nonsense is not the logical self-contradiction that sets faith against reason. As expressed in the *Fragments* it is a mistaken belief that one man could generate faith in another and so become like God for him. By this Climacus means that it is foolish to suppose that faith can be gained by mediation. This is nonsense not because it is a logical self-contradiction but because it is poorly thought out. In addition, Søe offers supporting evidence from the *Postscript* for the identification of nonsense with self-contradiction. However, in full context this passage assumes another meaning. Here follows the full passage:

A man arranges his life in a particular way which according to his knowledge of himself, his capacities, his faults, etc., is the most advantageous for him and hence also the most comfortable. It very well may be that this mode of life, and more especially his consistency in carrying it out, appears at the first glance or from many other viewpoint a ludicrous thing. If he is a presumptuous person, his eccentric mode of life will of course be proclaimed a higher understanding, etc. If, on the other hand, he is a serious man he will calmly listen to other people's views, and by the way he engages in conversation about it he will show

---

[1] *Critique*, p. 219.

that he himself can very well perceive the comic aspect it may have for a third party – and thereupon he will go home quite calmly and pursue the plan of life he had adopted as most suitable to him in view of the precise knowledge he has of himself. So it is also in the case of one who is really a Christian – if we remember that there is no analogy. He may very well have understanding (indeed he must have it in order to believe against understanding), he can use it in all other connections, use it in intercourse with other men. . . he will be able to see the point of every objection, indeed to present it himself as well as the best of them, for otherwise a higher understanding would in a suspicious way be a dubious promotion for stuff and nonsense. It is easy enough to leap away from the toilsome task of developing and sharpening the understanding, and so get a louder hurrah, and to defend oneself against every accusation by remarking that it is a higher understanding. So the believing Christian not only possesses but uses his understanding, respects the universal-human, does not put it down to lack of understanding if somebody is not a Christian; but in relation to Christianity he believes against the understanding and in this case also uses understanding. . . to make sure that he believes against the understanding. Nonsense therefore he cannot believe against the understanding, for precisely the understanding will discern that it is nonsense and will prevent him from believing it; but he makes so much use of the understanding that he becomes aware of the incomprehensible, and then he holds to this, believing against the understanding.[1]

Climacus rejects nonsense as applying to the Paradox. He does not reject it, as Søe implies, because it is self-contradictory in the logical sense, that is, against reason. He rejects it because nonsense is the attempt to portray something which is truly paradoxical as if it were rational to a person equipped with "higher understanding." Nonsense is the sham attempt to deny logical irrationality by postulating an ultimate rational understanding as possible. For Climacus this is a dangerous misunderstanding of Christianity, and to be rejected. Thus nonsense is the attempt to make rational what is not rational; this is rejected and quite rightly by reason itself. What then remains is the absurdity of the Paradox, the Incomprehensible, as distinct from nonsense. It is, as Climacus says again and again, a logical self-contradiction. To embroider it with "higher rationality," with an ultimate reasonableness, is to make nonsense of the Paradox.

(2) Even if nonsense were logically self-contradictory, which it is not, it is not possible to prove that the absurdity of the Absolute Paradox is therefore not logically self-contradictory. Two concepts may share certain characteristics and yet be different. Affirming their difference does not allow us to deny that there may be some characteristics in common. Even if it could be demonstrated that nonsense is logically self-contradictory this could constitute no proof that the Incomprehensible is therefore *not* logically contradictory.

[1] *Postscript*, pp. 503–4.

There are, then, two meanings of absurd. The distinction can be drawn by those who find in Climacus an opposition between true faith and reason. "Nonsense" is the attempt to deny the paradoxical quality of the Paradox. The Incomprehensible or true absurd is the logically self-contradictory. Indeed, it is difficult to see how those who deny the logical contradiction of the Paradox can make a distinction between the two meanings of Absurd.

Finally, Søe says that Climacus is "talking very loosely" when he says faith is against reason. This is curious. When one finds text which consistently denies an interpretation, the interpretation may nevertheless be correct; one might show this by demonstrating internal inconsistencies or a fundamental contradiction between premises. This, however, is not done.

This concludes Søe's arguments against the opposition of faith to reason. He then offers text from the *Journals* to support the thesis that faith is above reason. However, it is no proof that faith and reason do not conflict to show that faith is above reason. Traditional Kierkegaardian scholarship is tied to the metaphors of "above" and "against" and their supposed contrariety. I shall try to show this to be an inadequate understanding of Climacus' position. Having examined Søe's arguments attempting to deny a conflict between faith and reason I maintain the following conclusions as proven: (1) On the basis of unambiguous text found in the *Postscript* it is clear that the Paradox violates the nature of reason, that is, the Paradox is self-contradictory. (2) No arguments can be maintained against the proposition that the Paradox is a contradiction. Therefore I conclude that faith is against reason. If the text is unambiguous, the spirit, too, of the *Postscript* demands recognition. Surely there is no more important theme of the *Postscript* than its insistence upon the difficulty of becoming Christian. To reduce the self-contradiction of the Paradox and the tension this generates to the realm of the rationally compatible, possible, or even probable is to reintroduce an easy rapprochement between Christianity and life. Christianity becomes easier, increasingly easier, and soon everyone once again is Christian. Climacus' task is to make Christianity difficult, certainly not any more difficult than it is, but to demonstrate the fear and trembling of Christianity. If now there is no opposition between reason and faith, if now possibility and probability become the watchword for Christianity, we have, as Climacus says, confused the pagan and Christian realms.

Having demonstrated the opposition between faith and reason in the *Postscript*, I will attempt to prove the following arguments: (1) faith is above reason. Climacus' final position is, then, that faith is both against and above reason. (2) This is not a self-contradictory position. No understanding of the *Postscript* is possible so long as out of the argument, faith being both against and above reason, one forces an exclusive disjunct "above" *or* "against." Traditional Kierkegaardian scholarship divides itself into these two camps. I shall attempt to provide a solution which transcends both of these positions.

(1)
   A true sentence of Hugh of St. Victor: "In things which are above reason, faith is not really supported by reason, because reason cannot grasp what faith believes; but there is also a something here as a result of which reason is determined, or which determines reason to honor faith which it cannot perfectly understand."
   That is what I explained (for instance, in the Concluding Postscript). . .[1]

                                                              The *Journals*.

   The Paradox violates the laws of reason. Reason therefore can never accept the Paradox as rational. This has been established. Reason, however, can be made aware of its own limits. In the *Postscript* this is indicated by the cryptic but highly significant criticisms of reason offered by Climacus and expounded in the second chapter of this work. Since reason is limited to the logical sphere only, it cannot make judgments about the reality or existence of the Paradox but only about its rationality. Faith, therefore, is above reason in the sense that the Paradox may exist even when found to be irrational. The Paradox is for reason the symbol of its limits. In confronting the Paradox reason knows it to be irrational but not therefore impossible. It is the Paradox that reveals that *irrationality is not equivalent to existential impossibility and rationality is not equivalent to reality or existence.* When reason examines the Paradox, it has extended itself to its very limits, that is, to the recognition of the arbitrariness of its presuppositions and the realization that something may be beyond it. It must find the Paradox to be against reason since the Paradox is self-contradictory. However, having discovered its limits we must admit that, since reason cannot determine existential facts, it cannot say that the Paradox cannot be. Reason must, when confronted with the Paradox, understand that it cannot understand. In this sense the existence of the Paradox may be marked by terms of possibility, probability, improbability, etc., all indicating the disparity between reason's certainty of the irrationality

[1] *Critique*, pp. 185–6.

of the Paradox and its mere suspicions about the existence of the Paradox. When reason realizes its limits we can say that reason is "against" faith and yet that faith is "above" reason.

A more precise notion of the role of reason for Climacus can now be suggested. The laws of identity, contradiction, and excluded middle constitute the essence of reason. They are denied in the affirmation of the Absolute Paradox. Thus faith is against reason. But in confronting the Paradox reason can become conscious of its own limits. It is restricted to the realm of the logical. Thus reason can point beyond itself in the sense that it can realize that it can go no further, that there may be something more, that anything more goes against its laws, and yet that there may be such a thing.

Text supporting the opposition of reason to faith is unequivocal. Yet Climacus' criticisms of reason in the *Postscript* as well as text from the *Journals* supporting the notion of faith above reason is also clear. To maintain that Climacus subscribes to both is necessary.

(2) Yet Climacus is not inconsistent. There are no arguments to be found in the *Postscript* which deny that reason is against faith, none to oppose the thesis that faith is above reason. The two notions are not contrary; they refer to different aspects of reason, faith against reason, indicating reason's right to judge rationality or irrationality, faith above reason, indicating reason's recognition of the impossibility of judging the reality of that which denies reason. For Climacus reason is against faith and faith above reason.

CHAPTER 5

THE CHRISTIAN PURPOSE SERVED BY THE
"POSTSCRIPT"

Climacus' insistence upon the absurdity of the Paradox offers a way of maintaining the Christian nature of God; it allows the expectation that God will satisfy our desire for eternal happiness. The God of the Paradox is available for religious purposes. This must be proved.

Climacus says between man and God there is complete incommensurability. God – the Paradox – breaks our understanding; He is wholly Other: "... as between God and a human being... there is an absolute difference. In man's absolute relationship to God this absolute difference must therefore come to expression, and any attempt to express an immediate likeness becomes impertinence, frivolity, effrontery, and the like."[1]

Since God is Other, no restrictions based on the rules of reason can be placed upon His nature. God's nature – as Paradox – is not limited by the structure of our own thought. Reason, based on presuppositions that are valid in this world, cannot be applied to the realm of the Paradox, which has no necessary analogy with this world. To claim to have any knowledge of God's nature is to judge the Other by rational criteria; yet the Paradox makes reason's use illegitimate.

An unknown God, however, would seem to be unavailable for religious purposes. In the history of theology, however, there have been attempts to gain an understanding of this Other by various rational techniques. If God is Other we can frame some notion of His Being by subtracting from Him what we are, adding to Him what we are not. If God is Other, He (a) *must not be* what we are, and (b) *must be* whatever we are not.

(a) The doctrine of *via negativa* attempts to give some character to our understanding of God by eliminating from Him all human imperfections; since He is Other, He cannot be what we are; we are finite;

[1] S. Kierkegaard, *Concluding Unscientific Postscript*, Princeton, N.J., Princeton University Press, 1941, p. 369.

hence He is not finite. We are small and petty; therefore, God is not small and petty, etc. By elimination we derive some idea of God's Being. This has important consequences; to know what is not God frees us from worshipping a false God, that is, a God who possesses human characteristics. For example, if God were jealous, it would be necessary for us to satisfy the demands of this jealous God; to know that jealousy, a human imperfection, cannot be attributed to God makes it unnecessary to appease such a God. (b) If God is Other, then whatever we are not He must be. We are not perfect, we are not good, we are not truthful, therefore God must be perfect, good, and truthful. From this theory of opposites we gain an understanding of God's nature.

Such an understanding of God, gained through a theory of opposites and negation, however, assumes what Climacus denies, namely, that there is some necessary bond between man and God. It assumes that since God is Other He *cannot* have human characteristics but *must* have non-human ones. This implies that both man and God share rational standards of possibility and impossibility. To infer God's nature on the basis of negation and opposites is thus fallacious; it is to assert that God is the logical opposite of man, but by being so He is made to obey the laws of logic. God, the Other, is made into a being who is entirely comprehensible to man. Predictable and available, He is invoked by the simple rational operation of opposition. He is brought before us by thinking the opposite of whatever we are, or are not. The supremacy of rational thought is asserted; it forces God into the mold of our rational standards.

If, however, "God as Other" means God is the Paradox, then adding to or subtracting qualities from God's nature because they are the opposite of human qualities is an illegitimate extension of reason's power. It fixes God to the structure of our thought. God, the Other, is beyond our reason, and hence, for us He can be anything, including the Unlimited-limiting-Himself by being evil, good, finite, or all or none of these possibilities. The concept of God as the Paradox means that we can neither gain an understanding of Him directly by inspection nor indirectly by negation and opposition. The absolute difference between man and God is God as Paradox; there are no attributes that *must* be applied to Him. God's nature may be anything; we cannot know. The designation "absolutely different" or "other" stands, then, for the breakdown of *our* reason in the face of the Paradox. It must not become a subtle way of characterizing God, for then, through negation and opposition, we worship the convex face of our concave judgments about the nature of reason, that is, speculating about God but in reality talking only about ourselves and our rational limitations. From the Paradox anything is possible. The only testament to the God relationship is our awareness of the impossibility of understanding God; all else is ambiguous. Events in the life of man, misfortunes or successes, are not to be taken as signs indicating God's interest or displeasure in man, or to characterize Him in any way: "For if a human being cannot know with certainty whether a misfortune is an evil (the uncertainty inherent in the God-relationship as the form for always giving thanks to God), then he cannot know with certainty whether his good fortune is a good."[1]

It is an incommensurability best expressed in man's consciousness of *his* nothingness: "... self-annihilation is the essential form for the God-relationship... Religiously it is the task of the individual to understand that he is nothing before God..."[2] Thus, we cannot know whether God will reward or punish us for being subjective, that He has come into the world to save us, or whether He is indifferent to our suffering.

Yet, it is precisely this ambiguity that allows Climacus to postulate a Christian God. He can have the expectation that God is good and that He came into the world to relieve us of our suffering and to satisfy our desire for eternal happiness. If God's nature is incomprehensible to man, His nature *may be* exactly as Climacus describes it. We cannot know His nature; hence the Christian expectation is a legitimate possibility, which neither empirical nor *a priori* reason can deny. Since God is Other, He may be anything; He may, therefore, be a God to whom we can pray, fearsome yet loving, just but merciful. In the *Postscript* Climacus predicates a God with the following attributes: (1) He is a God who inspires fear in man: "They are busy about getting a truer and truer conception of God but seem to forget the very first step, that one should fear God."[3]

(2) He is fair, refusing to make invidious distinctions between the contemporaries of Jesus who witnessed this miracle and those who follow: "... contemporaneity is of no avail; because there can in all eternity be no direct transition from the historical to the eternal, whether the historical is contemporary or not. So to single out the

---

[1] *Postscript*, p. 399.
[2] *Postscript*, p. 412.
[3] *Postscript*, p. 484.

contemporary generation for special favor would also be a boundless injustice against those who came after..."[1]

(3) He came into the world in order to suffer: "The paradox is that Christ came into the world *in order to suffer*. Take this away, and then an army of analogies takes by storm the impregnable fortress of the paradox."[2]

(4) He is a God who has created man yet does not need him: "...God needs no man. It would otherwise be a highly embarrassing thing to be a creator, if the result was that the creator came to depend upon the creature."[3]

(5) For God the world is a system viewed by Him *sub specie aeterni*, even if for human beings it is not: "And finally, the reality of the world-historical evolution is not denied, but reserved for God and eternity, having its own time and place."[4]

(6) He is an elusive God, but only because He wishes to keep men from error, forcing them to reach Him by their own efforts, which, although painful, enables them to achieve the truth by a personal testing: "Nature is, indeed, the work of God, but only the handiwork is directly present, not God. And why is God elusive? Precisely because He is the truth, and by being elusive desires to keep men from error. The observer of nature does not have a result immediately set before him, but must by himself be at pains to find it..."[5]

The Paradox is not without content. By the end of the *Postscript* Christian attributes are joined to the Paradox; these merge logically into the traditional Christian picture of God that follows in Kierkegaard's religious works.

Climacus' expectation of God's nature is justified, but only in the sense that it may correspond to the nature of God. We cannot know. Any expectation, however, is as good as any other *if* God is the Paradox. God may foreordain suffering for all but the chosen few. He may be a malicious deceiver. He may be a jealous God. All expectations of God's nature are equally possible when we have shown reason to fail and realize in Paradox there can be no guide; there are only speculations, all equally possible. None can be either affirmed or denied rationally. In embracing the Paradox any notions of God's nature can be accepted, including, although not exclusively, Climacus' concept of God's Christian nature.

---

[1] *Postscript*, p. 89.   [2] *Postscript*, p. 529.
[3] *Postscript*, p. 122.   [4] *Postscript*, p. 142.
[5] *Postscript*, p. 218.

Having shown that Climacus' concept of God as Absurd is way of maintaining God's nature as Christian, I will now demonstrate that his concept of the Paradox and the incommensurability between man and God serves Christian purposes since he sees clearly that it is the *only* consistent way of maintaining God's nature as Christian. To minimize the folly of being Christian is to destroy the possibility of being Christian. A rational, non-absurd God is not Christian because (1) He is limited, and therefore not a Christian God, and (2) He is pantheistic, and therefore not a Christian God. (3) Finally, the postulation of a rational, non-absurd God rests upon an unproved assumption of reason; hence reason cannot legitimately speculate about God's nature and thus we are left with the impossibility of establishing a God by rational means.

(1) A God who can be understood is a limited, not a Christian, God. A rational God cannot be perfect; for to be perfect is to be omnipotent and to be omnipotent is to be bound by nothing, yet to be bound by the laws of reason is to be bound by something. A rational God, obeying the laws of reason, even if of His own making, is a limited Being, therefore not the Perfect Being of Christianity.

Spinoza and Anselm, in admitting that there are things God cannot do, deny that this limits Him. As Spinoza says: "We grant that God can create nothing more. And... we would say that we admit that if God should not be able to create what can be created it would contend against his omnipotence, but by no means if he could not create that which is self-contradictory..."[1] Anselm says: "How he is omnipotent, although there are many things of which he is not capable."[2]

The traditional rational solution: God possesses omnipotence, but without necessarily displaying it. He is under no obligation to produce everything, but must only be able to do so. As Descartes says: God has the power to deceive. Being good, however, He would not use this power.[3]

Thus, if omnipotent, God must be able to create even the irrational or the paradoxical, for without the power to do absolutely everything God might be omniscient, but could not be all-powerful. Since God's infinite power is not established in this lawful world, if God possesses

---

[1] B. Spinoza, *Short Treatise on God, Man and Human Welfare*, La Salle, Ill., Open Court, 1909, p. 15.

[2] St. Anselm, *Proslogium; Monologium; An Appendix in Behalf of the Fool by Gaunilon; and Cur Deus Homo*, La Salle, Ill., Open Court, 1951, p. 12.

[3] Descartes, *Philosophical Works*, New York, Dover, 1955, volume 1, p. 172.

omnipotence, it must exist potentially. God could have, but chose not to create, an irrational world; He still can. Therefore He is lawful and yet omnipotent.

It is absurd, however, to say of a rational God that He is not fully actual, but potential. Actuality must be a part of a rational God's perfection; it is a defect to make God or any part of Him exist potentially.

God is pure actuality expressing His essence fully. For God to hold aspects of Himself in reserve, that is, to be in part potential, is to allow the possibility that God may change, that He may reveal Himself in differing forms, so that, for example, the God of a hundred years from now may be a different and perhaps more infinite Being than the God of today. But this is absurd, for if He were or could be other than He is now He would not now be fully infinite. But He is; therefore, God must be fully actual and could have created His effects in no other manner; He has no power to change what He has created.

Thus, an infinite Being, if omnipotent, expresses His omnipotence; to be only potentially omnipotent is a rational impossibility for a most Perfect Being. But God's power in this world is, as we have seen, confined to the manifestation of His necessary laws. The world is rational, and the only power that God exhibits is action in conformity with omniscience. God has no power to change the rational confines of the world. He cannot be other than lawful. Power, then, is restricted to the bounds decreed by reason. But therefore, God is not all-powerful, but all-reasoning, having only power commensurate with rational necessities.

When God is rationally conceived, two Christian predicates of God, actuality and lawfulness, make impossible a third Christian predicate, omnipotence. Since omnipotence cannot exist in God potentially, an infinite God being necessarily actual, and since law is the ruling characteristic of this world, God, not having the power to defy law even potentially, is not omnipotent. Any combination of two of three Christian predicates of Perfection – omniscience, omnipotence, and actuality – makes the third impossible. If we insist that God be omnipotent and yet lawful, He cannot be wholly actual; if God is omnipotent and actual, He cannot be fully lawful; if He is lawful and actual, He cannot be omnipotent.

If we postulate a non-paradoxical God of reason, we are forced to eliminate from His nature necessary Christian attributes. To accept a rational, non-absurd God is to be left with a limited, not a Christian, God.

(2) A God who can be understood by human reason is not a Christian God, but a pantheistic God, which, for Climacus, is the only "consistent position outside of Christianity." Spinoza shows consistently the consequences of affirming a rational, non-absurd God.

If God is perfect there can be no action in space and time; to act is to do something not yet done, but if there is something not yet done there is a lack, and God, having that lack, could not be perfect. But God is perfect; therefore, God cannot act in space and time. This, however, makes absurd His having a Son, intervening in history, or acting upon men's prayers. The Christian concept of God as Father must be rejected as contradictory – if we admit a rational God obeying the laws of reason.

Again, to understand the meaning of God is to admit that there can be only one such Being. A plural number of Gods is impossible, for these Gods would, by their very presence, limit and define each other, making it impossible to conceive of any one solely through itself. One cannot conceive of either one of two existing Gods without limiting both, for one prevents the other from extending His omnipotence infinitely. But it is absurd to suppose that God is limited. Therefore God must be one. Therefore no Trinity, no concept of the plurality of the God-head is possible.

Furthermore, if God obeys the laws of reason, God to be Perfect must contain everything, for if He did not, He would be finite, having something outside of Himself which by being outside would set limits upon His Being. Since God is omnipotent, nothing can exist outside of Him; yet there are human beings; therefore they too must be within God. Man is a mode of God, and therefore subject to the same Divine Law as are all other parts of nature which comprise His Being. He has no special place in nature. The Christian concepts of sin, judgment, and salvation, which separate man from nature, must be discarded – given a rational, non-absurd God.

Finally, with a non-paradoxical rational God there can be no freedom: that Being, than which nothing greater can be conceived, must order nature with inflexible control. There are no exceptions to this rule; if any were allowed, the demonstration of the Perfection of God would rationally fail, for then something would exist independently of God, thereby limiting Him. But nothing can limit the Perfect. Therefore, all nature obeys rational law. As Spinoza says: "That He has supreme right and dominion over all things, and that He does nothing under compulsion, but by His absolute fiat and grace. All things are bound to obey Him, He is not bound to obey any."[1] Man too must act in accordance with the "fixed and immutable order of nature," and cannot transgress God's causative action. Every action performed by man is determined, as are all other actions, by all other modes. Man's "freedom" is illusory. Man, then, has no freedom to choose or reject Christ, but only affections and compulsions which determine his denomination.

Therefore, as illustrated by Spinoza's critique, a concept of God as non-absurd, that is, one who is rational and can be understood rationally, makes impossible the Christianity of Jesus Christ. To use reason in religion is to deny the Christian God, replacing Him with an immanent, indwelling, amoral being: *deus sive natura*.

(3) All rational attempts to comprehend God's nature assume a resemblance between cause and effect, an assumption which is unwarranted: Invoking reason to characterize God's nature necessitates a statement of community between cause and effect. This statement is unjustified; reason is unable to speculate validly about God's nature.

To talk accurately about God's nature requires that the assertions we make about Him truly correspond to His Being. Since inspection of God is closed, there is no direct way of knowing that our assertions truly correspond to His Being. There is, however, an indirect justification which is twofold:

(a) By the Thomists: the terms we use in describing the nature of the finite world accurately can be used to describe the nature of God accurately. God's Being must correspond to the world He creates, that is, He must Himself contain, at the very least, the same qualities He creates. Thus, in understanding accurately this world we can make assertions about God that truly correspond to His Being. Father Copleston says: "It is a fundamental principle with St. Thomas that the perfections of creatures must be found in the Creator in a supereminent manner, in a manner compatible with the infinity and spirituality of God. For example, if God has created intellectual beings, God must be possessed of intellect; we cannot suppose that He is less than intellectual."[2] This enables the Thomists to make assertions about God's Nature which correspond to His Being since the two realms, finite and infinite, are fundamentally similar, this fundamental simi-

---

[1] Spinoza, *Theologico-Political Treatise* in *Philosophical Works of Spinoza*, New York, Dover, 1955, p. 187.

[2] F. Copleston, *A History of Philosophy*, London, Burns Oates & Washbourne Ltd., 1950, p. 357.

larity having been established because one was caused by the other and so must be like that other, different only in degree.

It is conceivable, however, that a cause might be wholly unlike its effect, sharing nothing significant in common with it, what the Thomists call an equivocal cause. How do we determine that there is a resemblance between an infinite cause and its finite effect, and thus a correspondence between our assertions and God's Being? We do this only by having an absolutely clear idea of the resemblance between man and God. Revelation justifies the Thomistic doctrine of resemblance between cause and effect. In Genesis: "And God said, Let us make man in our image, after our likeness: and let them have dominion over the fish of the sea, and over the fowl of the air, and over the cattle, and over all the earth, and over every creeping thing that creepeth upon the earth... So God created man in his own image, in the image of God created he him..."[1]

Analogy is valid – for the faithful. For the rational, there has been no necessary demonstration of a resemblance between cause and effect, and thus no justification for the necessary correspondence between our assertions of God's Being and His Being.

(b) The second justification of necessary resemblance between cause and effect has been offered by Spinoza to justify our assertions about God's being. As with the Thomists a necessary resemblance between cause and effect is asserted. Unlike the Thomistic position it attempts to justify this assertion by reason.

Spinoza argues that our terms, used in the finite realm, can apply to the infinite as well. The finite, caused by God, must have something in common with its cause. The similarity between the two allows us to know the nature of God. When we understand adequately the finite world we gain some understanding of God. Proposition III, Book I, of the *Ethics* asserts that a cause must have something in common with its effect: "Prop. III. – If two things have nothing in common with one another, one cannot be the cause of the other. Demonst. – If they have nothing mutually in common with one another, they cannot (Ax. 5) through one another be mutually understood, and therefore (Ax. 4) one cannot be the cause of the other. – Q.E.D."[2]

From God's effects, created within and about us, we are able to discern traces of the nature of God; we are able to have a necessary, that is, true idea of God, and use terms accurately to describe His

---

[1] Genesis I: 26, 27.
[2] Spinoza, *Ethics*, New York, Hafner, 1953, Bk. I, Prop. III.

Being, since our being and the terms we use to describe our world accurately correspond to His Being.

That the cause may have nothing significant in common with its effect and that therefore it is not necessary that the terms we use, even if clearly and distinctly conceived, necessarily correspond to the Infinite was first suggested by Oldenburg in a letter to Spinoza. Oldenburg questioned the necessity of Prop. III, Bk. I of the *Ethics* or Axiom IV in the early draft of the *Ethics* with which Oldenburg was acquainted: "The fourth axiom, namely, 'Things which have nothing in common cannot be one the cause of the other' is not so obvious... as to need no further light for its illumination. For God has nothing essentially in common with created things, yet He is held by almost all of us to be their cause."[1]

Spinoza answers justifying the assertion of resemblance between cause and effect: "... it follows that things which have nothing in common between them cannot be one the cause of the other. For when the effect has anything in common with its cause, then whatsoever it might have, it would have from nothing."[2]

Spinoza's justification is: a thing is either self-caused, that is, comes from nothing, or is caused, that is, comes from something. We shall concern ourselves with the caused since the finite is caused. If an effect has nothing in common with its cause, the effect must have come from nothing, for if one thing is caused and the other is its cause there is, at the very least, the bond of an asymmetrical relationship of causation between them, and therefore something in common between them. But the effect could not have come from nothing, for we have said we are concerned with the caused, which, by definition, must have come from something. There is, then, something in common between cause and effect.

What Spinoza fails to establish, however, is a significant similarity between cause and effect which would allow us to justify a correspondence between our assertions of God's Being and God's Being, since by knowing God's *effects* we know God's *Being*. This failure is made evident by inspection of the term "common." It is true that if there is nothing in common between cause and effect one could not have come from the other, for to say that one thing has nothing in common with another is to say that there is no relationship between the two. Being caused, however, implies a relationship; therefore,

---

[1] *The Correspondence of Spinoza*, London, Allen & Unwin, 1928, p. 79.
[2] *Correspondence*, p. 83.

there must always be something in common between a cause and its effect.

But all cause and effect need have in common is a causative relationship: one is the cause, the other the effect. That is enough to establish the necessary relationship between the two without showing any significant resemblance. Even equivocal causes have something in common with their effect, namely, the relationship of causing and yet being wholly different from the caused. Spinoza has not proved that the resemblance established in the relationship between cause and effect is enough to allow us to infer that through either the other can be understood. He has proved that there must be something in common between cause and effect, but the similarity discovered is trivial. It does not allow us to assert that we can apply our terms to the Infinite since we have not established any significant resemblance between the finite and infinite realms. The terms we use may not correspond to God's Being since the infinite realm may not resemble the finite. We cannot know, for we do not know that we share anything significant in common with the Infinite.

In conclusion, the only sustained rational attempt to justify our assertions about God fails. We do not know whether the finite realm, even if caused by God, has anything significant in common with the Infinite. Therefore, our rational assertions about God's nature are unjustified; they may not necessarily correspond to His Being.

The only justification of the correspondence of our assertions and God's Being is arbitrary, being either a postulate of faith or the true but trivial argument used by Spinoza. There may be no correspondence but only equivocation. The statement of resemblance between cause and effect cannot be treated as a self-evident axiom of thought; it is not open to empirical inspection and cannot be accepted simply because faith postulates it. It is not supported by rational argument.

Indeed it is the real possibility of an equivocal cause that makes fallacious the supreme rational attempt to prove God, the ontological argument. The argument fails not because it transports real existence into pure thought, but because it presumes God's nature to be what human beings consider perfect. Even if God is Perfect, He may be different from our meaning of the term perfection. If so, the proof, which regards existence as a necessary perfection, fails; it may be only our limited idea of what constitutes perfection and have no resemblance to God's perfection. If God is than which nothing greater can be conceived, conceivably it would be a greater God who is not conceivable by limited human beings. Therefore God, greater than can be conceived, need not have any of the attributes, including existence, which we give Him; they may only be limitations upon His Being. Between man and God equivocation may reign. Anselm says this: *"He is greater than can be conceived*. Therefore, O Lord, thou art not only that than which a greater cannot be conceived, but thou art a being greater than can be conceived. For, since it can be conceived that there is such a being, if thou art not this very being, a greater than thou can be conceived. But this is impossible."[1] The ontological argument does not prove the existence of God but shows the infinite distance between man's limited intellect and God. It is a religious exercise designed to humble human reason.

Rational modes of knowing God's nature rest upon an arbitrary assumption that there is a resemblance between cause and effect. Without proving this we are not rationally entitled to use our terms, originating in the finite, to characterize the Infinite. Furthermore, even *if* we grant a necessary resemblance between cause and effect and *if* we postulate a non-absurd God, we prove a pantheistic, not a Christian, God, and a limited, not a Christian, God. Attempting to understand God by rational means denies His Christian nature. There is no need, however, to grant these postulates; hence all rational attempts to expound the nature of God fail.

Climacus' insistence upon absurd faith is the only consistent way of allowing traditional Christian predicates to be attributed to God. Only Climacus' attack on rational theology makes the venture to believe in a *Christian* God reasonable. If God is the Paradox, reason cannot deny God's nature as Christian. If God is not the Absurd, reason proves the non-Christian nature of God. Climacus' Paradox is a rational attempt to save the Christian God by pointing out the limits of reason.

This position, of course, is not new; it has, however, the merit of being quite clearly recognized by Climacus. The danger in allowing the realm of faith to be infected by reason was first stated precisely by Tertullian:

These are "the doctrines" of men and "of demons" (I Tim. 4 : 1) produced for itching ears of the spirit of this world's wisdom: this the Lord called "foolishness" (I Cor. 3 : 18, 25), and "chose the foolish things of the world" to confound even philosophy itself. For [philosophy] it is which is the material of the world's wisdom, the rash interpreter of the nature and the dispensation of God. Indeed

---

[1] *Proslogium*, chaps, XV, XVI.

heresies are themselves instigated by philosophy ... Unhappy Aristotle! who invented for these men dialectics, the art of building up and pulling down; an art so evasive in its propositions, so far-fetched in its conjectures, so harsh in its arguments, so productive of contentions – embarrassing even to itself, retracting everything, and really treating of nothing! ... From all these, when the apostle would restrain us, he expressly names *philosophy* as that which he would have us be on our guard against (Col. 2 : 8)... Away with all attempts to produce a mottled Christianity of Stoic, Platonic, and dialectic composition! We want no curious disputation after possessing Christ Jesus, no inquisition after enjoying the gospel! [1]

It remains now to inquire why the *Postscript* fails to be *fully* Christian.

---

[1] Tertullian, "On Prescription Against Heretics," in L. Harold De Wolf, *The Religious Revolt Against Reason*, New York, Harper and Row, 1949, p. 41.

CHAPTER 6

THE ANTI-CHRISTIANITY OF THE *"POSTSCRIPT"*

The demonstration of the anti-Christianity of the *Postscript* rests upon two arguments: (1) Christianity is made a relative, not an absolute, end. (2) By Climacus' own dialectic Christianity becomes an objective truth, no longer an affair of the spirit.

(1) It is necessary to determine the nature of the relationship between subjectivity, the desire for eternal happiness, and Christianity, the expectation that one's eternal happiness is to be found in Jesus Christ. Specifically, the problem is to investigate whether subjectivity and Christianity share equally privileged positions of worth or whether, despite the appearance of a harmonious directorate, there is a single and ultimate value in the *Postscript* to which all other values are subordinate and from which they gain their justification. It is my thesis that there is an important difference in the values assigned to subjectivity and Christianity, that Climacus is primarily a subjectivist, and that, therefore, his position in the *Postscript* is anti-Christian, for one cannot be both a subjectivist (existentialist) and a Christian. The demonstration of this thesis consists of three parts: (a) Christianity and subjectivity are different. (b) Subjectivity, not Christianity, is the ultimate end in the *Postscript*. (c) The subjectivity of the *Postscript* is anti-Christian and thus must be considered by the Christian as an imperfect stage to be overcome. This thesis, if correct, might explain Kierkegaard's use of pseudonym. If the *Postscript* is not Christian it is less than his final position, and it is reasonable to offer this work, as Kierkegaard did all his pre-Christian writings, under another's name. Why the *Postscript* is not a final Christian position will now be demonstrated.

(a) There are grounds for suggesting that subjectivity and Christianity are identical. This interpretation is made possible by passages in the *Postscript* linking the two terms by the copula "is" as: "sub-

jectivity *is* Christianity." There would, then, be no problem in identi-
fying the ultimate value in the *Postscript*: Christianity or its synonym,
subjectivity. The passages that follow contain examples which link
the two terms with the copula "is":

Christianity is spirit, spirit is inwardness, inwardness is subjectivity, subjectivity is essentially passion, and in its maximum an infinite, personal, passionate
interest in one's eternal happiness.[1]
. . . for Christianity is precisely an affair of spirit, and so of subjectivity, and
so of inwardness.[2]
Now if Christianity is essentially something objective, it is necessary for the
observer to be objective. But if Christianity is essentially subjectivity, it is a
mistake for the observer to be objective.[3]
But suppose Christianity were nothing of the kind; suppose on the contrary
it were inwardness. . .[4]

The interpretation which makes the copula bear the meaning of
exact synonymity is, however, untenable. Christianity is defined by
Climacus as the Paradox – and nothing else: "The last thing that
human thinking can will to do, is to will to transcend itself in the
paradoxical. And Christianity is precisely the paradoxical."[5]

The Paradox gives no advice: it cannot suggest a world-system or
offer us a methodology of truth. These speculative embroiderings upon
the Paradox Climacus denies as approximations: "Christianity is no
doctrine concerning the unity of the divine and the human, or concerning the identity of subject and object; nor is it any other of the
logical transcriptions of Christianity... Christianity is therefore not
a doctrine, but the fact that God has existed."[6]

The Paradox states Jesus as Christ existed; it does not say that
infinite concern is good or that the Paradox is subjectivity. Subjectivity, the true way to the Paradox, is not identical with the Paradox. The copula "is" in the occurrences in the text cited should be
interpreted as stating not exact synonymity but rather inclusion in
the Aristotelian sense. To say "is" means that A is included within
or is part of the class B. To say "Christianity is subjectivity" means
that to be a Christian is to be in passion; not any kind of passion,
however, but a type of passion produced by the Paradox. Socrates'

---

[1] S. Kierkegaard, *Concluding Unscientific Postscript*, Princeton, N.J., Princeton University
Press, 1941, p. 33.
[2] *Postscript*, p. 42.
[3] *Postscript*, p. 51.
[4] *Postscript*, p. 193.
[5] *Postscript*, p. 95.
[6] *Postscript*, pp. 290–1.

passion, for example, is great, but not yet the degree of subjectivity demanded of the Christian.

Since there can be passion and inwardness which is non-Christian as with Socrates, subjectivity and Christianity cannot be strictly synonymous: "That subjectivity, inwardness, is the truth; that existence is the decisive thing; that this was the path along which it was necessary to move in order to approach Christianity, which is precisely inwardness, though not any and every type of inwardness..."[1] Christianity is only part of the class of the subjective, although it is the highest part; but the highest is not identical with the whole. Therefore, subjectivity and Christianity are not synonymous but represent two different values.

Having established a difference between inwardness and Christianity it is necessary to determine whether Climacus is primarily a subjectivist, a Christian, or both in equal measure.

(b) That for which everything is done is the highest end, that is, has the greatest value. That which is done for the sake of another is an inferior value in the hierarchy of goods. As Aristotle says: "... we call what is pursued as an end in itself more final than what is pursued as a means to something else; and what is never chosen as a means we call more final than what is chosen both as an end in itself and as a means; in fact, when a thing is chosen always as an end in itself and never as a means we call it absolutely final."[2]

With these definitions I shall examine Climacus' system, investigating reasons given for being subjective and Christian, thereby seeking to determine the dominant value in the *Postscript*.

To ask a question of the form "why should I be x" is to seek reasons for being or doing something "x." Answers to questions of this form are made by showing that x is necessary to or follows from a "B" which is accepted as final. An example: "why should I be good"; an answer: "because if you are not, you will be punished." Here goodness, a secondary value, is justified by being asserted as a necessary condition for gaining freedom from punishment, in this example, the final end. But a question of the form, "why should I be x," cannot be applied to the final end. A value that is final cannot be justified by reference to anything else. It is either compelling or not. Aristotle says: "Similarly we ought not in all cases to demand the 'reason why' (*aitia*);

---

[1] *Postscript*, p. 251.
[2] Aristotle, "Nicomachean Ethics" in *Wheelwright's Aristotle*, New York, Odyssey Press, 1951, p. 167.

sometimes it is enough to point out the bare fact. This is true, for instance, in the case of 'first principles' (*arche*); for a bare fact must always be the ultimate starting-point (*arche*) of any inquiry."[1]

Subjectivity in the *Postscript* is absolute. The question "why should I be concerned with my eternal happiness" is not raised. Subjectivity is not justified in terms of anything else but justifies everything else. If the individual accepts subjectivity, there are many arguments in the *Postscript* to demonstrate that only by being in total subjectivity is he not deceiving himself in his life affirmation. Indeed, the major portion of the *Postscript* is concerned with the important but secondary consideration of ways to attain a fuller subjectivity. But there is no justification of subjectivity itself; nor can there be any. The only answer to the question "why should I be subjective" is the denial of the logical form of the question indicating thereby the absolute quality of this value: "you should be subjective because you should." In the *Postscript* subjectivity is supreme: "And if initially my human nature is merely an abstract something, it is at any rate the task which life sets me to become subjective...."[2]

If, however, one asks the question: "why should I be Christian" the *Postscript* provides an elaborate justification. There is no way to understand the Paradox; it is absurd; any attempt to explain it misunderstands and corrupts, thus changing it. Nevertheless, there is very good reason for accepting the unintelligible Paradox: be Christian *because* Christianity leads to the highest passion or subjectivity which is necessary in order for us to gain our eternal happiness: "... this is precisely what the paradox says; it merely thrusts the understanding away in the interests of inwardness in existing"[3]; "Christianity does not lend itself to objective observation, precisely because it proposes to intensify subjectivity to the utmost...."[4]

Further corroboration is found early in the *Postscript*. Here the use of Christianity and the Paradox as means and not as an end is specifically made: "I, Johannes Climacus... assume that there awaits me a highest good, an eternal happiness... I have heard that Christianity proposes itself as a condition for the acquirement of this good, and now I ask how I may establish a proper relationship to this doctrine."[5]

---

[1] *Nichomachean Ethics*, p. 170.
[2] *Postscript*, p. 149.
[3] *Postscript*, p. 195.
[4] *Postscript*, p. 55.
[5] *Postscript*, p. 19.

Climacus is passionately interested in his eternal happiness; Christianity offers him eternal happiness. In infinite zeal he proposes to follow Christianity. One is Christian believing in the Paradox *because* it leads to something else. But choosing the Paradox because it leads to something else is to make Christianity less than the dominant value, for it is done not for its own sake but for the sake of another – subjectivity or the desire for eternal happiness. But, "That for which everything is done is the highest end, that is, has the greatest value. That which is done for the sake of another is an inferior value in the hierarchy of goods." Subjectivity, professed for its own sake, is the highest value in the *Postscript*; Christianity, offered for the sake of subjectivity, is of secondary value. Subjectivity, not Christianity, is the final end of the *Postscript*.

(c) To be primarily subjectivist or existentialist is to be profoundly anti-Christian in both the conventional *and the Kierkegaardian* meanings of the term.

A Christian is one who believes in Jesus as Christ, offering his obedience because God commands, not because he is rewarded for doing so. Obedience for the sake of some end, such as eternal happiness, prevents one from being truly religious – not because there is no reward in being Christian – but because being a Christian for the sake of the reward is immoral, a turning of the final end, the Paradox, into a means toward some other end. Kant's statement of religious obligation is definitive of the orthodox Christian position: one must do his religious duty because he must, not because it proves to be in his interest to do so. [1] Interest and benefit in acting religiously are not precluded, but must never be decisive.[2]

Climacus, faced with the problem of gaining his eternal happiness and confronted with a Christianity that offers it, nevertheless must not accept the Paradox *because* it gives it to him. It is this failure to keep the Paradox an absolute end that makes the *Postscript* less than Christian.

Climacus knows a final end must be final: "All relative volition is marked by willing something for the sake of something else, but the highest end must be willed for its own sake. And this highest end is not a particular something, for then it would be relative to some other particular and be finite."[3]

---

[1] Kant, *Critique of Practical Reason*, Chicago, University of Chicago Press, 1949, p. 52.
[2] *Critique of Practical Reason*, pp. 59, 61.
[3] *Postscript*, p. 353.

Yet Climacus professes Christianity for the sake of subjectivity: "Let the individual merely take note of his own mode of existence and he will know it. If the idea of an eternal happiness does not transform his existence absolutely, he does not stand related to it; if there is anything he is not willing to give up for its sake, the relationship is not there."[1]

Climacus is then Christian *because* it serves the final end. This denies the meaning of the absoluteness of the Paradox for both the orthodox, as represented by Kant, and *Kierkegaard*: God is to be obeyed whether or not He fulfills our infinite expectations. As Kierkegaard says in *Edifying Discourses*:

And when the easy play of happiness beckoned you, have you thanked God? And when you were so strong that it seemed as if you needed no assistance, have you thanked God? And when your allotted share was small, have you thanked God? And when your allotted share was suffering, have you thanked God? And when your wish was denied you, have you thanked God? And when you must deny yourself your wish, have you thanked God? And when men did you wrong and offended you, have you thanked God? We do not say that the wrong done you by men thereby ceased to be a wrong, for that would be an untrue and foolish speech! Whether it was wrong, you must yourself decide; but have you referred the wrong and the offense to God, and by your thanksgiving received it from Him as a good and perfect gift? Have you done this?[2]

The choosing of Christianity for its rewards also violates precepts set by Climacus early in the *Postscript*: "... God may require everything of every human being, everything and for nothing."[3]

Climacus, affirming the Paradox because he wants eternal happiness, postulates the right deed but for the wrong reason; this is his religious offense. The justification for acceptance of the Paradox, then, is not the eternal validity of the Paradox itself – Climacus' analysis of reason as approximate prevents him from attaching traditional notions of objective goodness, truth, or reality to the Paradox. Nor is it his desire to affirm God in spite of objective evidence to the contrary. It is done for the sake of gaining his eternal happiness. This is as destructive of the Paradox as is the attempt to understand it; in either case the absoluteness of the Paradox vanishes. Furthermore, using the Paradox as a means to an end violates Climacus' insistence upon the infinite distance between man and God: "Precisely because there is an absolute difference between God and man, man will express his own nature

[1] *Postscript*, p. 352.
[2] S. Kierkegaard, *Edifying Discourses*, New York, Harper & Row, 1958, pp. 42–3.
[3] *Postscript*, p. 122.

most adequately when he expresses this difference absolutely."[1] The separation between man and God is falsely scaled when He is made an instrument to serve human purposes. This is to make God relative to our purposes. To make relative, however, is to treat familiarly; God, the Absolute Other, cannot be treated familiarly. Therefore God cannot be made relative to our subjective interest and still be for us wholly Other.

What appears in the *Postscript* is the anti-religious motive for being religious. It is as harmful to Christianity as an end-in-itself as are self-interest arguments commonly offered for being religious. Climacus attacks these arguments, since they make Christianity easier by holding out temporal rewards.[2]

Climacus warns that venturing to believe is strenuous; so strenuous that suffering is the mark of the person in faith: "... it is precisely a sign of the relationship to the absolute that there is not only no reward to expect, but suffering to bear";[3] "... let me rather know from the beginning that the road may be narrow, stony, and beset with thorns until the very end; so that I may learn to hold fast to the absolute *telos*... but not led astray by calculations of probability and *interim* consolations."[4]

But suffering can be for a purpose and rewards come at many stages. Christianity is made as difficult as possible – "until the very end," only to offer delayed but ultimately forthcoming bonuses (the possible realization of *eternal* happiness) if one is only patient enough to suffer Christianity. The difference between self-interest arguments for the acceptance of Christianity and Climacus' argument is the degree of strenuousness needed; there is no difference in their reduction of the Paradox and Christianity to a subordinate position.

The true religious spirit has great, even infinite, expectations; it does not accept or obey God because of these expectations. God is to be obeyed because He is, not because He rewards us. He is: "I AM WHO AM," not "I AM THAT WHICH BRINGS YOU ETERNAL HAPPINESS." Climacus, viewing Christianity as an aid to his subjectivity, neither understands nor makes the final movement of faith. To attain true Christianity the *Postscript*, for all its valuable lessons on the meaning of religion, must be overcome, that is, the Paradox embraced as an end-in-itself. Climacus' Christianity is not yet strenuous enough. Soon

[1] *Postscript*, p. 369.
[2] *Postscript*, p. 361.
[3] *Postscript*, p. 360.
[4] *Postscript*, p. 362.

after the completion of the *Postscript* Kierkegaard abandons pseudo-nym; he must also abandon the primacy of subjectivity and move to total Christianity; anything less is paganism.

(2) The final religious error of Climacus is his failure to understand the structure of his own movement; while recognizing the essence of faith to be irrational, Climacus, instead of introducing the highest uncertainty and suffering, presents Christianity in a reasonable light, that is, a choice which a reasonable man could accept.

It is my thesis that the venture to believe in the Paradox of Jesus Christ, rather than an "act of madness," is a cunning and rational movement, one entirely plausible to a man of reason. The demonstration of this involves the following steps: (a) Gaining our eternal happiness is a rational and speculative problem. (b) Believing in the Paradox of Jesus Christ as the answer to the rational problem of eternal happiness is a rational and speculative answer. (c) Venturing to believe not in the Christian Paradox but in speculative reason is the highest absurdity.

(a) The problem of eternal happiness is a rational and speculative one. Climacus' concern for his eternal happiness relies upon an acceptance of speculative reason which is not allowed him by his criticism of speculative reason. Subjectivity is concerned with the future (eternal happiness) as opposed to merely the present. But if the entire apparatus of speculative-historical reason is to be rejected, so also must be the form of the question which it introduces: a concern about future consequences instead of present living. Only the rational man can inquire about a non-temporal eternity. Only with speculative, systematic reason is it possible to maintain that some indefinite, eternal happiness is more important than present, temporal happiness. This attempt to live for one's eternal happiness is the essence of rational activity. Climacus' sacrifice of the existential present to serve the eternal future is symptomatic of a prudent and speculative nature. In even asking the question of eternal happiness existence is sacrificed to theory.

(b) The answer given by Climacus to the rational problem of gaining one's eternal happiness – belief in the Paradox – appears to go against reason; it does not. My thesis is: the Paradox is not absurd *if* reason is approximate; on the contrary, the flight to the Absurd is rational. The argument has the following form:

(i) Speculative reason makes judgments about existence. Yet the critical part of reason, surveying the mode of its metaphysical pretensions, reveals that this mode is only approximate. Reason is limited; it must limit itself, that is, set boundaries for itself.

(ii) Thus reason cannot arrive at eternal truths in regard to existential problems, for to accept abstract principles as valid in our existence in time is unreasonable. If reason is approximate, its judgments have validity only in the epistemological or logical realm; judgments by reason about existence must, then, logically be disregarded. Judgments such as "objectively absurd" and "rationally impossible" as applied to existential commitments are injudicious; what transcends reason's province is beyond the capacity of reason to judge.

(iii) There is, then, nothing inherently absurd or logically contradictory in accepting any non-rational way which claims to satisfy our concern about the eternal. If reason is limited, it is rational or at least not irrational to venture to accept any non-rational means that promises eternal happiness. Without reason we lack all standards of truth and falsity. But if there are no rational standards, then the acceptance of the Paradox through a non-rational mode cannot be considered an act of absurdity in which one undergoes the "crucifixation of the understanding."[1] Kant in the *Critique of Pure Reason* states a similar position:

Whenever I hear that a writer of real ability has demonstrated away the freedom of the human will, the hope of a future life, and the existence of God, I am eager to read the book, for I expect him by his talents to increase my insight into these matters. Already, before having opened it, I am perfectly certain that he has not justified any one of his specific claims; not because I believe that I am in possession of conclusive proofs of these important propositions, but because the transcendental critique, which has disclosed to me all the resources of our pure reason, has completely convinced me that, as reason is incompetent to arrive at affirmative assertions in this field, it is equally unable, indeed even less able, to establish any negative conclusion in regard to these questions.[2]

(iv) Furthermore, the venture to believe is not merely non-rational. The acceptance of the Christian Paradox is the best movement open to a rational individual who wants his eternal happiness enough to make a leap to something that may possibly give it. Not to leap is to have no chance at it, since it is to remain in reason, which by our admission of its limitations forfeits any possibility of our obtaining eternal happiness through it. The leap, then, does not deny reason, but is done with the realization that, since abstract reason is limited,

[1] *Postscript*, p. 500.
[2] N. K. Smith, *Immanuel Kant's Critique of Pure Reason*, London, Macmillan and Co., 1950, p. 602.

we ought therefore to accept its opposite, the Paradox. Since abstract reason does not answer our concern, perhaps non-reasonable claims do; and perhaps they do. Since reason must be restricted to the speculative realm and not extended to existence, the decision to embrace its opposite is a rational movement dictated by our desire to discover eternal happiness. As Pascal indicated, given the stakes, the limitations of reason, and the possibility of finding eternal happiness by venturing, it makes good sense to leap. Pascal says:

> Let us then examine this point, and say, "God is, or He is not." But to which side shall we incline? Reason can decide nothing here. There is an infinite chaos which separated us. A game is being played at the extremity of this infinite distance where heads or tails will turn up. What will you wager? According to reason, you can do neither the one thing nor the other; according to reason, you can defend neither of the propositions.
>
> Do not then reprove for error those who have made a choice; for you know nothing about it. "No, but I blame them for having made, not this choice, but a choice; for again both he who chooses heads and he who chooses tails are equally at fault, they are both in the wrong. The true course is not to wager at all."
>
> Yes, but you must wager. It is not optional. You are embarked. Which will you choose then? Let us see. Since you must choose, let us see which interests you least. You have two things to lose, the true and the good; and two things at stake, your reason and your will, your knowledge and your happiness; and your nature has two things to shun, error and misery. Your reason is no more shocked in choosing one rather than the other, since you must of necessity choose. This is one point settled. But your happiness? Let us weigh the gain and the loss in wagering that God is. Let us estimate these two chances. If you gain, you gain all, if you lose nothing. Wager, then, without hesitation that He is.[1]

The conclusion for both Climacus and Pascal: it is reasonable to wager on God.

The rationality of Climacus' leap of faith may also be compared with that of Kant. Kant's analysis of human knowledge reveals the limitations of reason when reason is used in a transcendent manner rather than when confined to its proper transcendental function, that is, reason must be employed in categorizing intuitions, not in speculating upon matters which go beyond our sense data such as the metaphysical quest for God and eternal life. In the "Antinomy of Pure Reason" Kant demonstrates both that the world has had a beginning in time and that it could not possibly have had such a beginning in time, that everything is simple and that nothing is simple, that there is freedom and God and that there is no freedom and no God. This demonstration proves that reason fails to answer our existential concern, since transcendental reason cannot deal with matters

---

[1] B. Pascal, *Pensées*, New York, Modern Library, 1941, p. 81.

of eternal concern and reason empty of sense data can prove anything. This makes trivial the activity of pure, transcendent reason; it is a system in which a thing is as true as its opposite and is therefore worthless. By allowing everything and prohibiting nothing all results are equally true, equally attainable, equally trivial.

Since reason is limited and cannot legitimately speculate about the existence of God, freedom, and immortality and yet since God, freedom, and immortality are needed for human life, it is rationally permissible to predicate them as existing. This postulation, although not demonstrable, *may* have its counterpart in reality. Since this postulation is necessary for human life, we *should* act as if it does exist; it might:

> I do not at all share the opinion which certain excellent and thoughtful men. . . have so often been led to express, that we may hope sometime to discover conclusive demonstrations of the two cardinal propositions of our reason – that there is a God, and that there is a future life. On the contrary, I am certain that this will never happen. For whence will reason obtain ground for such synthetic assertions, which do not relate to objects of experience and their inner possibility. But it is also apodeictically certain that there will never be anyone who will be able to assert the *opposite* with the least show [of proof], much less, dogmatically. For since he could prove this only through pure reason, he must undertake to prove that a supreme being, and the thinking subject in us [viewed] as pure intelligence, are *impossible*. But whence will he obtain the modes of knowledge which could justify him in thus judging synthetically in regard to things that lie beyond all possible experience. We may therefore be so completely assured that no one will ever prove the opposite, that there is no need for us to concern ourselves with formal arguments. We are always in a position to accept these propositions – propositions which are so very closely bound up with the speculative interest of our reason in its empirical employment, and which, moreover, are the sole means of reconciling the speculative with the practical interest.[1]

For Climacus as for Kant a critique of pure reason makes impossible any negative judgments upon the existence of the Paradox.

The demonstration that belief in the Christian Paradox is a reasonable gamble is based upon the argument that *if* historical-speculative reason fails to attain our eternal happiness, the denial of the historical-speculative in the leap of faith may reveal truly the nature of the Real which is closed to reason and its judgments. This is Kant's conclusion. This is also the logical movement that Climacus makes; the charge most pertinently brought against him is that he is too clever, not that he is an irrationalist. He frames his problem in accordance with reason's *telos*, not on feeling's natural interest in immediate, temporal ends.

---

[1] *Critique of Pure Reason*, pp. 595–6.

And he chooses to act rationally: leap when reason cannot tell him what to do. But to leap at anything when reason admits its limitations, is to give us some real chance at finding eternal happiness; refusing to do so nullifies any chance to succeed. As William James says: "I do not wish... to forfeit my sole chance in life of getting upon the winning side, – that chance depending, of course, on my willingness to run the risk of acting as if my passional need of taking the world religiously might be prophetic and right."[1]

The rationality of Climacus' leap is apparent. Hegel is right: "That those living processes of individuals and nations, by seeking and satisfying their own limited ends, serve at the same time as the means and tools of something higher of which they know nothing and which they therefore accomplish unconsciously – this could be questioned. ... As against this, I have proclaimed at the outset that reason rules the world..."[2] The cunning of reason insinuates itself into even seeming irrationality. Climacus' movement is rational; reason remains and not an irrational venture to believe in an Absurd Paradox.

There are, then, two movements in the *Postscript*. First, the movement in which Climacus attacks reason, but where, if he has done his work well, he is left with a Paradox which is not at all irrational to embrace, since if reason fails to attain his eternal happiness, passion and irrationality may. Correction of this demands rejection of the second part of the *Postscript* – that the highest suffering and greatest uncertainty is entailed by the Christian Paradox. The second movement is Climacus making the leap as difficult as possible, talking about the necessity of crucifying the understanding, and maintaining a belief in the Paradox of Jesus as Christ in spite of reason. This demands a rejection of the first part of the *Postscript* – the critique of reason, since the Paradox is absurd only if reason's judgments against it are valid.

Either Climacus abolishes the first movement of the *Postscript* or the second. To keep the criticism of reason, it is necessary to reject the notion of madness in accepting the Christian Paradox; to keep the Paradox of Jesus as Christ as being truly absurd it is necessary to abandon the criticism of reason. In the *Postscript* the dilemma is unresolved.

(c) A conclusion that allows for Climacus' critique of reason and his insistence upon a truly absurd venture in order to be in true faith is

---

[1] William James, *Will to Believe*, New York, Longmans, Green, and Co., 1911, p. 27.
[2] G. W. F. Hegel, *The Philosophy of Hegel*, New York, Modern Library, 1954, p. 16.

the following: the greatest absurdity, the highest faith, and most strenuous venture is to realize rationally the absurdity of reason's pretensions, yet nevertheless, *in spite of this knowledge*, venture to believe in the discredited claims of reason to gain for us eternal happiness. Any other belief in any other absurdity is simply a disguised probability judgment or shrewd gamble; only the absurd acceptance of the traditional claim of reason to fulfill our eternal happiness, already shown by skeptical reason to be absurd, is not a disguised but clever gamble. Therefore choose to believe – in reason. This is the highest and most absurd faith. Curiously, this coincides with the doctrine of the rationalist who accepts reason – but for entirely different reasons. Absurd faith in reason in spite of our recognition of its inability to reach eternal happiness is the only true act of faith, faith defined as venturing to believe in an objective impossibility with the most passionate inwardness. Therefore, be rational.

Conclusion

The *Postscript* is a stage in the movement to Christianity. It shows the passionate and irrational to be the core of religion and the conscious acceptance of the absurd to constitute religious faith. To structure religion rationally and to defend it logically is only to reveal its deliberate thoughtlessness and folly.

Climacus' movement, however, is imperfect. Making Christianity a means, not an end, he violates the absoluteness of religion. In attempting to show the Paradox as the absurd and irrational, he succeeds only in making Christianity a good gamble. The *Postscript* is a stage to be overcome in the movement to Christianity.

INDEX

172-D